HS5318: Scope of Human Services

Judith Lewis/ Marianne Woodside/ Tricia McClam/Thomas Packard/ Michael Lewis

CENGAGE
Learning™

Australia • Brazil • Japan • Korea • Mexico • Singapore • Spain • United Kingdom • United States

HS5318: Scope of Human Services

Judith Lewis/ Marianne Woodside/ Tricia McClam/Thomas Packard/ Michael Lewis

Executive Editors:
Michele Baird

Maureen Staudt

Michael Stranz

Project Development Manager:
Linda deStefano

Senior Marketing Coordinators:
Sara Mercurio

Lindsay Shapiro

Senior Production / Manufacturing Manager:
Donna M. Brown

PreMedia Services Supervisor:
Rebecca A. Walker

Rights & Permissions Specialist:
Kalina Hintz

Cover Image:
Getty Images*

* Unless otherwise noted, all cover images used by Custom Solutions, a part of Cengage Learning, have been supplied courtesy of Getty Images with the exception of the Earthview cover image, which has been supplied by the National Aeronautics and Space Administration (NASA).

© 2008 Cengage Learning

For product information and technology assistance, contact us at
Cengage Learning Customer & Sales Support, 1-800-354-9706

For permission to use material from this text or product,
submit all requests online at **cengage.com/permissions**
Further permissions questions can be emailed to
permissionrequest@cengage.com

ISBN-13: 978-1-4266-4980-6

ISBN-10: 1-4266-4980-0

Cengage Learning
5191 Natorp Boulevard
Mason, Ohio 45040
USA

Cengage Learning is a leading provider of customized learning solutions with office locations around the globe, including Singapore, the United Kingdom, Australia, Mexico, Brazil, and Japan. Locate your local office at:
international.cengage.com/region

Cengage Learning products are represented in Canada by Nelson Education, Ltd.

For your lifelong learning solutions, visit **custom.cengage.com**

Visit our corporate website at **cengage.com**

Cengage Learning purchased [enter business unit name] from Thomson on July 5, 2007

Printed in the United States of America

Facing the Challenges of Management

CHAPTER OUTLINE

The Need for Managerial Competency

The Purposes of Human Service Programs

Functions of Human Service Management

Planning

Designing the Program and Organization

Developing Human Resources

Supervising

Managing Finances

Monitoring and Evaluating

Human Relations Skills

Decision-Making Skills

Leadership and Change Management: Keeping the Organization Responsive and Vibrant

The Multicultural Organization

Summary

Discussion Questions

Group Exercise

Case 1: Transitions into Management

References

1

What do we mean when we talk about human service organizations and the ways in which they should be managed? An organization can be any group of people—large or small—working together to achieve common goals. In a *human service organization,* however, these goals are always focused on improving the lives of the people being served. The organizations that share this goal of life enhancement can vary tremendously, from the tiny storefront agency, to the multifaceted community organization, to the statewide public service department. Managers and service deliverers certainly work toward the enhancement of human development in many ways and many settings, but their shared focus on human development brings with it a common outlook, a mutual set of problems, and the need for an approach to management that may differ from the business models in the profit-making environment.

Human services are delivered in the context of the *human service agency.* An agency is a human service organization that is designed specifically to provide services to the community. Examples of human service agencies include the following:

- Mental health facilities;
- Specialized agencies that deal with specific problem areas (for example, addiction, legal problems, or family problems);
- Population-oriented agencies that deal with specific groups of people (for example, child welfare agencies or agencies serving an elderly population);
- Career, employment, or rehabilitation agencies that provide opportunities for individuals to gain skills that will help them attain positive career growth and economic security;
- Educational institutions. (The term *agency* is not usually used for educational institutions. However, schools do provide human services to their students and communities and share organizational characteristics with other human service organizations. The skills involved in developing and managing programs in educational settings and community agencies share many similarities.)

Within a human service agency, we often find a number of programs. A *program* has a smaller scope than a human service agency or institution and might be developed within a larger agency in order to meet specific needs. For instance, a mental health center might have a special program for families of children with mental illness, or an agency providing employment services might have a special program for people who have been unemployed for a long period of time.

Especially at the program level, management becomes a major concern not just for agency directors and supervisors but also for the people who see themselves primarily as professional service providers. Human service professionals used to hesitate at the thought of being managers, assuming that a management position would cut them off from the lifeblood of day-to-day work with clients. Unfortunately, this stereotype led many human service providers to avoid becoming competent in management for fear that they might somehow be turning their backs on their clients or losing their professional identification as helpers. Today, however, more and more professional helpers have come to recognize the importance of having management skills, even if they have no plan to change their job titles or career goals.

Management can be defined rather simply as the process of (1) making a plan to achieve some end, (2) organizing the people and resources needed to carry out the plan, (3) encouraging the helping workers who will be asked to perform the component tasks, (4) evaluating the results, and then (5) revising plans based on this evaluation. This process can be shared by managers and by people who currently and essentially identify themselves as human service professionals.

Today most people recognize that awareness of managerial functions is important in any human service organization. Many professionals find themselves in supervisory roles because such positions in human service agencies and institutions are normally filled by people with training in the helping professions. Even professionals who spend all their time in direct service delivery need to understand how their organizations work so that they can implement new ideas, help improve operations, and influence others to make needed changes.

After reviewing some examples of the need for managerial competency in human service organizations, this chapter will discuss the concept of organizational purpose as a unifying principle and outline key management functions. These management functions are bound together by leadership, so the chapter goes on to address the human relations and decision-making skills that underlie effective leadership. Leadership and change management will be presented as ways of involving all staff in the accomplishment of organizational missions, goals, and objectives and ensuring the ongoing viability of the organization. In today's environment, organizations must demonstrate multicultural competence, so the concept of the "multicultural organization" is addressed.

THE NEED FOR MANAGERIAL COMPETENCY

Everyday incidents tend to remind professional helpers that they must learn how to manage people, programs, and resources, if only to safeguard the humanistic, people-centered orientation that should permeate human services. Many human service workers are being forced to choose either to participate actively in the administration of their own programs or to leave leadership in the hands of others who may have little understanding of the helping process. Some may find that their choice is to learn to manage their own programs or lose them altogether.

The following incidents—all typical of the kinds of conflicts professional helpers face every day—speak for themselves.

KEITH MICHAELS

As soon as he had earned his master's degree, Keith Michaels decided to put all his time and energy into creating a center that would serve the youth of his community. Now in the fifth year of its existence, that center has grown from a storefront office in which Keith saw a few walk-in clients into a major community center, complete with recreational facilities, a peer counseling project, an ongoing consultation program, a busy staff of individual and group counselors, and a major role in the local youth advocacy movement. Most of the clients, counselors, and community members involved with the center are convinced that the explanation for this growth lies in the fact that the staff has always been close to the community's young people and responsive to their needs. They feel that Keith, with the help of the energetic staff he has recruited, can realize a dream they all share, and they want his promise that he will stay with the center as director.

Keith is hesitant, for the agency no longer "runs itself" the way it once did. There is a need to departmentalize, to organize staff hiring and training, and to lay out appropriate plans for further change. Keith is afraid to place the management of the center solely in the hands of a professional administrator because he fears that the community responsiveness that has been a hallmark of the program might be lost. He wants to continue to have an effect on the center's future, but he knows that if he becomes the center's director he will have to learn how to plan, organize, and budget on a larger scale.

SHIRLEY LANE

Shirley Lane has spent several years working in a community agency for developmentally disabled adults. She has developed an approach for working with her clients that she has found highly effective, and she knows that her approach might be helpful to others. In fact, it would provide a major innovation in the field if research showed it to be as effective as she thinks it is.

Because her approach is so promising, Shirley has consistently been encouraged to submit a proposal for federal funding. Finally, her proposed project is being funded; she will now have the chance to implement a training and research project that can make a significant contribution to the field. She knows, however, that if the project is to be successful, she must develop effectiveness in planning projects, supervising the trainees who will help carry out the project, maintaining the budget, and evaluating the results of interventions. She can meet this challenge only if she can successfully carry out the required managerial functions.

BILL OKITA

As the harried director of a small community mental health project, Bill Okita never has enough time. He spends half his time in direct service, working with individuals and groups, and this is an aspect of his job that he would not want to give up. He finds his work with clients to be a positive part of his workday; it is what keeps him going and makes all his efforts worthwhile.

Bill has a small staff of professional service providers, all of whom are highly competent. Perhaps this high level of competence accounts for the dramatic rise in the number of clients. The project now has a waiting list for appointments, which conflicts with Bill's belief that counseling should be readily accessible for community members. Yet the agency's funding does not allow Bill enough financial resources to hire additional counselors. He has to make do with the present staff members, but they are all stretched too thin as professionals.

Bill has just been approached by a local citizens' organization whose members are interested in serving as unpaid volunteer counselors at the center. If they could participate in this way, Bill's time problems would be solved. He would finally have enough personnel available to provide the immediate service that he thinks counselees should have. With the pressure off, he could still devote some of his time to providing direct services instead of having to spend all his time dealing with pressing administrative problems and fund-raising.

Bill has no doubt that these volunteers could do an effective job of serving clients if he provided training and supervision. It is his own skill in supervising and coordinating their efforts that he questions. In fact, he recently turned down the opportunity to have doctoral-level psychology students complete internships at the center because he was not sure that he could handle their needs. Now, however, the situation has become desperate. He needs the help of these volunteers, but he must be able to train, supervise, and coordinate them. If he performs his managerial functions more effectively, he can spend less time on them.

LILLIAN SANCHEZ

Lillian Sanchez began her career as an elementary school teacher. She spent many years working with young children and found the work fantastically rewarding. Yet, when she received training as a counselor, she wanted the chance to experience that side of helping, too. She accepted a position as a high school counselor because her city did not employ school counselors at any other level.

That work, too, has been fulfilling. But Lillian has always wished that she could combine the rewards of working with young children with those of working as a counselor. She feels that elementary school is the place where effective counselors should be working, for only at that level might there be a chance to prevent the personal and educational problems her high school clients all seem to be facing.

Suddenly, Lillian has the opportunity of a lifetime. A new elementary school is being built in her area, and the potential principal, a longtime professional colleague, has asked her to join the staff as the district's first elementary school counselor. She will build her own program in the direction she thinks best and perhaps have the chance to consult with other schools in the development of additional programs. Lillian has no doubt that this position would be a dream come true. She has always wanted to counsel at the elementary school level, and now she can create a truly innovative program based on the concept of prevention.

Still, she hesitates. She knows she can counsel the children effectively, but she does not know whether she can build a program where none existed before. She will need to learn how to plan effectively, how to provide leadership for teachers and parents, how to consult beneficially with other counselors, and how to evaluate her own efforts. The only way she can have the opportunity to practice her child-counseling skills is to develop administrative skills at the same time.

DAVID WILLIAMS

David Williams is one of a group of human service workers conducting a preventive program under the auspices of a child and family service center. In recent years, the financial situation of the center has changed. The agency is being forced to cut back services in some areas to maintain adequate funding for other programs.

David and his colleagues have been called into the executive director's office and told that, as much as she appreciates their fine work, their program might be eliminated within the next year or two. The director recognizes that the preventive program is very popular in the community; calls have been coming in constantly from schools, churches, and recreational centers to request assistance from it. Although she knows that the program is doing something right, she does not know just what it is. She does not know how important it is in comparison with the functions being performed by workers providing direct, clinical services to troubled families.

David and his colleagues now have a real challenge before them. They know that they are helping the community; the informal feedback they have been receiving from young people, parents, and community agencies tells them that. They also know that right now they have no way of proving it, no way of showing that the prevention program is accomplishing something important. They have a short time in which to prove themselves, and they know that their only chance is to plan their program on the basis of goals that the administration agrees are important, to coordinate their efforts with those of other programs, and to develop an accurate evaluation method. If they are going to survive, they need to learn how to carry out these tasks. In short, they need to be able to manage.

Keith Michaels, Shirley Lane, Bill Okita, Lillian Sanchez, and David Williams are all typical human service professionals. They are not interested in changing their professional identities or in moving up some administrative ladder. They are interested in improving and enhancing their human service delivery systems. It could be argued that they should not make the professional move they are contemplating. Perhaps Keith should turn over the management of his counseling center to someone whose original training was in business administration. Possibly Lillian should stay at the high school level, where she can spend all her time on direct service, and wait until the program is fully established by someone else before moving into an elementary school situation. Conceivably, David and his fellow human service workers should seek employment at an agency where preventive programs are already appreciated and where they would have no pressure to prove themselves or to sell their program.

If they do make these decisions, however, they should make them freely, based on their evaluation of all the possible options and their values, priorities, and professional judgment. They should not be in the position of having to choose inaction just because they lack the skills needed to bring about change either in their careers or in their programs. This book is intended to provide human service workers and students with basic management knowledge that may help them in their current jobs or prepare them to take on managerial work. Human service organizations will be presented as complex, purposeful organizations with the potential of bettering social conditions and enriching the lives of employees, clients, and community members.

THE PURPOSES OF HUMAN SERVICE PROGRAMS

Human service programs deal with the personal and social development of individuals, families, and communities. Sometimes they enhance this development through the provision of direct services such as education, training, counseling, therapy, or casework. Often they work indirectly, through consultation, advocacy, referral, information dissemination, community development, or social action. The ultimate purpose of these programs, regardless of the methods used, is to enhance the well-being of clients or consumers. In one study addressing excellence in human service organizations (HSOs), Harvey (1998) found that *purpose* was the dimension of

FIGURE 1.1
THE COMPONENTS
OF ORGANIZA-
TIONAL PURPOSE

Source: *Performance by Design: Sociotechnical Systems in North America* by Taylor & Felton, ©1993. Reprinted by permission of Prentice-Hall, Inc., Upper Saddle River, NJ.

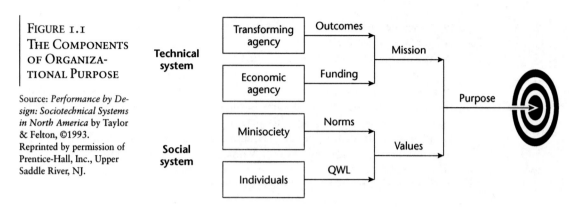

excellence that was cited most frequently by survey respondents. According to Harvey, "having a very clear sense of purpose, direction, mission, or vision and a focus on its accomplishments is necessary to achieve excellence in an HSO" (p. 37).

Taylor and Felten (1993) have defined an organization's purpose as the "business mission of the system and its philosophy of human values" (p. 39). They see an organization as having four interactive and interdependent elements (see Figure 1.1). First, an organization is a transforming agency, which produces outcomes of value. In the case of human service organizations, people (clients or customers) are typically transformed, from individuals, groups, families, or communities with needs or problems to those with needs met or problems ameliorated. Second, an organization is an economic agency, which either produces a profit or, in the case of governmental or not-for-profit agencies, maintains a balanced budget or surplus. Third, an organization is a mini-society, with norms and a culture that guide members' behavior and indirectly impact organizational effectiveness. Finally, an organization is a collection of individuals who each have unique values, beliefs, needs, motivational profiles, expectations, and skills.

The first two elements, concerning performance and fiscal health, compose an organization's mission: its distinct competencies and reason for existence. The second two elements address organizational norms and member quality of working life (QWL) and shape the organization's philosophy and values. Purpose, then, is the combination of mission and values: it tells the organization's employees, clients, community, and larger environment why it exists, what it will focus on, and how it intends to treat its staff, clients, and community. Purpose in this sense, when fully articulated and regularly enacted, provides direction, energy, and vision for the organization's employees, who are engaged in a cooperative endeavor to enhance individual and community well-being in some way.

Managers, as leaders of an organization and stewards of its resources, must always maintain focus on the organization's purpose, designing systems and behaving in ways consistent with it. Management is a set of systems and processes designed to help employees accomplish organizational and individual goals. Rapp and Poertner (1992, pp. 277–278) have gone so far as to invert the traditional hierarchy, putting clients and direct service workers at the top and the director at the bottom. This setup suggests that the manager's job is to help workers get the job done, by clarifying expectations, providing necessary resources, and removing obstacles. In the demanding day-to-day life of a manager, it is important to keep this perspective and to resist the temptation to focus only on procedural issues or management needs without taking the time to evaluate organizational results. Management processes and leadership are both essential and should be jointly well executed, and this is a manager's contribution to the success of the organization.

FUNCTIONS OF HUMAN SERVICE MANAGEMENT

Currently, most human service programs are based either in public organizations, such as departments of social services and schools, or in nonprofit agencies that have been created to meet specific community needs. (Increasingly, for-profit organizations are entering this field, presenting new challenges to existing agencies to clearly achieve desired outcomes in a cost-effective manner while remaining true to professional standards, values, and ethics.) Whether programs provide direct or indirect services and whether they are housed in public or private agencies, they tend to share similar managerial functions. The management of human service programs includes the following major components:

- **Planning:** Developing visions for the future, creating strategy, setting goals and objectives for attaining them, and selecting program models
- **Designing:** Structuring and coordinating the work that needs to be done to carry out plans
- **Developing human resources:** Mobilizing the people needed to make the program work and taking steps to enhance their productivity
- **Supervising:** Enhancing the skills and motivation of service providers
- **Managing finances:** Planning the use of financial resources for reaching goals and controlling expenditures
- **Monitoring:** Tracking progress on program objectives and activities
- **Evaluating:** Comparing program accomplishments with the standards set at the planning stages; using the results as the basis for change

The force that binds together and energizes these processes is leadership: working with employees to articulate a vision, manage the external environment, oversee the design of organizational processes, link elements of the system together, create a supportive organizational culture, and manage change. This model is represented in Figure 1.2.

Human service professionals who know how to perform these functions can play important roles in managing their programs. They can make plans to achieve human service goals, organize the people and resources needed to carry out the plans, encourage and assist individuals delivering services, and evaluate the results.

FIGURE 1.2
A CONCEPTUAL
FRAMEWORK FOR
HUMAN SERVICE
MANAGEMENT

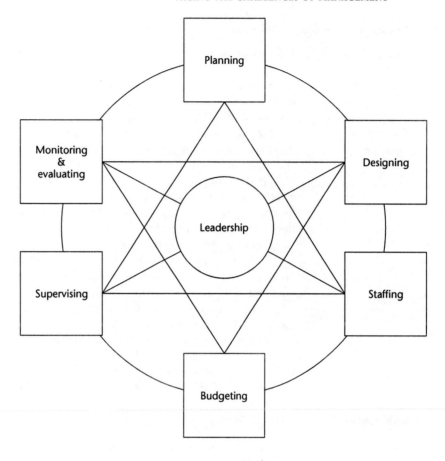

PLANNING

The planning process in human service settings begins with the assessment of community needs and visions of a desired future state, from a perspective that reflects the agency's purpose (mission and values). Planners use a variety of methods to determine what problems and opportunities exist within a given population and—just as important—what community members see as their most pressing priorities. If currently offered services are also analyzed, planners can recognize gaps in the human service system.

This assessment of needs and the identification of community strengths or assets (Kretzmann & McKnight, 1996) provide the basis for selecting the potential goals of the agency or program. Community members, potential consumers, and service providers, as well as policy makers, must all be involved in setting service goals. Actual programs, or collections of related activities, can be developed on the basis of these goals. Instead of assuming that a given activity should form the heart of a human service program, planners examine alternate methods for achieving the objectives that have been set. Only then can specific plans for service implementation be laid.

DESIGNING THE PROGRAM AND ORGANIZATION

If the planning function helps human service workers determine what should be accomplished, the designing function helps them carry out the plan. Designing is done at three levels: the organization as a whole, the program, and individual jobs. There are two aspects of design. First, structure is the element traditionally associated with the "organizing" function: what functions are in the various units and how the chain of command is set up. Second, design includes organizational processes such as communication and decision-making mechanisms. These are not apparent on the organizational chart but are crucial to effective functioning.

Furthermore, as will be explained in Chapter 5, design is both a noun and a verb. As a noun, it describes structure and processes; as a verb, it is the process for creating the organization—deciding what needs to be done and determining the best structures and processes. Organization design flows from the result of the planning phase: mission, goals, objectives, and overall strategies.

A design, or, as is more often the case, a redesign, of the organization produces the structure and processes that allow all people and units involved to understand what part they are to play in the organization, how ongoing communication and coordination of effort are to occur, and what the lines of authority and responsibility are expected to be.

Within these parameters, the possible types of structure vary tremendously, depending on the goals, needs, resources, size, and environment of the organization. They also vary in accordance with the values, philosophy, and theoretical approaches of the designers. These aspects will be discussed in Chapter 4.

DEVELOPING HUMAN RESOURCES

An organization's plans and design are put into operation by people: human service programs are labor-intensive. A major part of each budget goes toward salaries and benefits for service deliverers and support personnel. The success of services depends on the manager's ability to mobilize valuable human resources so that the immediate and long-term needs of the organization and its clients are met. Especially in times of retrenchment, when financial resources dwindle, human service managers must plan carefully both to bring needed people into the organization and to enhance their development once they have begun to provide services.

The development of human resources involves using the unique contributions that all of the workers of the human service enterprise can make. Special attention should be paid to the knowledge and skills that women and people of color bring to the organization (Asamoah, 1995; Bailey, 1995; Healy, Havens, & Pine, 1995). Feminist and transcultural perspectives, as represented by a diverse workforce, enhance the capabilities of human service programs to provide relevant and compatible services to diverse client populations.

Careful recruitment, selection, training, and appraisal processes should be used for both paid employees and volunteers. Hiring practices normally take into account the abilities, experiences, and characteristics of potential human service workers, but managers sometimes forget to consider the organization's unique needs. Job responsibilities and priorities should be defined precisely even before vacancies are advertised. This analysis should then form the basis for screening applicants and for hiring those candidates whose qualities best fit the actual jobs to be performed. After hiring, the new employee should be fully oriented to the agency in areas ranging from the governance structure and policies and procedures to agency history and organizational culture.

The environment and program activities of human service organizations change so rapidly that ongoing development of staff is essential. The function formerly known as "personnel and training" has recently been reconceptualized as "strategic human resource management," reflecting the principle that training and development should be guided by the key strategies, priorities, and programmatic needs of the agency. When an agency implements a new program or adopts improved service delivery methods, staff will need appropriate training. As will be discussed later, treating agencies as learning organizations (Senge, 1990) and encouraging lifelong learning on the part of staff are becoming increasingly common principles of staff and organization development. Beginning and advanced training in computer usage will become more necessary as agencies increasingly tap the potentials of the Internet, database management, and other software.

Once people have been hired, performance appraisals should occur regularly. They should be based on objective analyses of the tasks and behaviors that lead to successful job performance. Fair, objective performance appraisals serve dual purposes. They can be used for evaluating individuals and also for identifying areas of needed development in the individual or in the organization. Performance appraisals can point the way toward new behaviors that should be learned and practiced, allowing services to keep pace with client needs.

One way to expand an agency's human resources is to encourage volunteer participation. This approach works as long as recruitment and assignment of volunteer service providers are planned as carefully as is the hiring of professional employees. Volunteers can add significantly to a program's thrust because they provide fresh ideas and strong links to their communities. Community members' participation increases the agency's service delivery capacity, but only if these contributions are respected as highly as those of paid personnel.

SUPERVISING

Supervision involves helping a worker maximize his or her effectiveness in service delivery by providing support and encouragement, helping build skills and competencies, and overseeing the supervisee's work. The nature of the supervisory relationship depends on the supervisor's leadership style, the supervisee's motivation, and the organization's needs. In essence, however, the supervisor's primary task is to ensure that each supervisee (1) views his or her own work as a key component in helping the organization achieve its goals; (2) develops the knowledge, skills, and attitudes necessary for carrying out this work; and (3) remains motivated toward growth.

The supervisor encourages the development of professional excellence in his or her supervisees in the roles of clinical supervisor and educator. In

11

fulfilling all of the functions of the supervisory role, the human service manager provides, as a leader, emotional and psychological support to his or her staff as a means of preventing worker burnout and enhancing motivation and job satisfaction. Educational supervision, in addition, addresses workers' needs for professional growth and development in the provision of job-related services designed to improve client outcomes (Shulman, 1993).

The human service supervisor also fulfills a management, or administrative, function. As such, the supervisor must possess knowledge and skills relevant to the day-to-day direction and control of unit operations—for example, assigning and delegating work, coordinating workers' activities, planning unit goals and objectives, and so on. In addition, the supervisor must have a keen awareness of the agency's broader organizational and administrative concerns, including strategic and tactical planning, structure, staffing, fund-raising, budgeting, and program evaluation.

MANAGING FINANCES

Human service professionals can understand their own programs only if they know how they are budgeted. When they are directing specially funded projects, full-time service providers control the allocation of limited financial resources. Even when their programs make up only parts of total agency structures, human service workers should try to gain access to and understand the financial reports that affect them.

The process of setting and controlling the budget is closely related to planning and evaluation. In fact, a budget is fundamentally a program in fiscal terms. The more closely related the budget is to goals of people who hold a stake in the agency's success, the more effectively it is likely to work.

A budget must be seen as the concrete documentation of the planning process, bringing ideals into reality. An annual budget does not have to be based simply on a slight increment over the previous year's figures. Instead, it can reflect program goals and the costs of activities expected to attain those goals. For instance, zero-based budgeting requires that each set of activities be justified in its entirety before resources are allocated. Program budgeting places accountability on programs by allocating resources for the attainment of specific objectives rather than simply assigning funds to "line items" such as personnel costs or supplies.

Budget making is thus a decision-making process through which allocations are made to one service rather than another. If it is to be closely related to the program development process, human service providers should be involved. At the very least, they need to be aware of how the planning process has been translated into financial terms.

Even when traditional line item budgets are used, planners can ensure that the budget reflects program priorities by following careful procedures for allocating resources to specific activities. The objectives that have been set as part of the initial plan can be analyzed in terms of the activities that need to be performed before the objectives have been met. Each activity can then be broken down in terms of time span, personnel costs, and non-personnel costs until a total cost for the activity has been determined. The costs for these activities can be either budgeted according to program or placed in the context of a line item budget. In either case, the budget that finally sees the light of day is one that has been derived not from assumptions about what items should always be included in a budget but from analyses of program goals and priorities.

Once an effective annual budget is in place, ongoing financial reports help determine whether expenditures and income are as expected or whether significant deviations from the plan have occurred. The human service worker who understands the budget does not need to give it a great deal of attention after the initial stages. Managers, of course, need to pay attention to money matters when there are variances that need to be accounted for or acted on.

Closely related to budgeting is the whole question of funding mechanisms. Public agencies depend for their funding on legislative appropriations as well as other possible sources of revenue. Private, nonprofit agencies tend to depend on some combination of grants, contracts, contributions, and fees paid for services, either by clients or by third parties. For-profit companies operating in the human service field typically are funded by contracts and fees (often paid by third parties) and have the added benefit of using their own capital. The brand of funding can have a major effect on an agency's programs because funding sources vary in terms of long-range predictability and the services they tend to encourage. Program planners and budget makers need to be aware of the agency's major focus and should not lose sight of program goals when new funding possibilities appear. The integrity of agency goals is especially difficult to maintain in times of resource scarcity. At such times, it is most important to recall that budgeting and fund-raising should remain subsidiary to planning.

Monitoring and Evaluating

A program must have information systems to enable all staff to keep track of what is being done and accomplished. Such a system is variously referred to as "documentation," "keeping stats," or a "management information system." Such a system should keep track of not only program activities but also the ultimate outcomes, or results, as they relate to clients. Information systems are used both to track organizational activities and progress and to provide data for evaluation. Evaluating a program involves comparing program accomplishments with criteria and standards set at the planning stage. Evaluation is not necessarily a specialized activity carried on only at special times by outside experts descending on an organization. It should be seen as an ongoing self-assessment process in which all human service workers participate.

The agency's information system allows for a constant monitoring of agency activities and provides data for evaluation—an assessment of the effects of services on clients. Human service professionals need to know whether the services being carried out are in accordance with what was planned within a certain time and budget. They also need to know whether the program is meeting its objectives in terms of client change.

13

When criteria and standards are clear, evaluators can identify the data needed to measure the degree to which objectives have been attained. The next step becomes identifying the source of the data and designing a system for obtaining and reporting information.

If an ongoing information system is in place, evaluations of effort and effectiveness can be implemented either by external consultants or by agency workers. Once evaluation results have been reported, needed program changes can be identified and implemented.

It is difficult to separate evaluation from planning because an effective plan must include an evaluation component, but an effective evaluation must be based on the goals and objectives identified as part of a plan. Most important, human service professionals must be aware of the need to gather appropriate data as part of normal, ongoing program operation. Only then can evaluation gain its rightful place in the management and coordination of all activities. When this takes place, human service workers who already "know" that their services are effective will be able to prove it to others.

HUMAN RELATIONS SKILLS

Management is never a solo performance. It involves the orchestration of complex human elements into a whole that is characterized by harmony rather than discord. In any organization, managers must be able to work effectively with individuals and groups. They must encourage communication, build personal motivation, and form cooperative problem-solving groups. These interpersonal skills are as important in planning and budgeting as in direct supervision.

Effective application of all of the management functions just described requires polished interpersonal skills. If a plan is to be a living document, its formation must involve active participation of the people who will be affected by it, including potential service consumers as well as policymakers, board members, funding sources, managers, and agency employees. The human service professional who is involved in developing any program plan or innovation must be able to encourage and work closely with a variety of individuals and groups, each of whom might have a special priority in mind.

Budgeting requires far greater skill with people than with dollars and cents. Although the budget is closely involved with the planning process, it invariably attracts more conflict than any other planning component. Allocation of scarce resources means that funds are distributed to some programs, services, or individuals at the expense of others. Even when the most rational possible procedures are used to make the necessary decisions, both the processes and the results need to be sold to participants. When more traditional budgeting approaches are used, political processes and the balancing of conflicting interests come to the fore and need to be accepted as realities. No one can build a budget without being in close touch with the needs of funding sources, consumers, and workers.

The balancing of human and organizational needs is also important in creating an agency's structure. Organizing involves dividing and coordinating the efforts of individuals and departments. These tasks can be done successfully only if the manager is sensitive to the needs of the people contributing to the work effort. The degree of centralization or decentralization, of specialization or generalization, of control or independence built into the organization's structure is a function of the needs being met. These needs include both those dictated by the tasks to be performed and those dictated by the human characteristics of the people performing them. Like a plan or a budget, an organizational structure depends as much on interpersonal dynamics as on technical concerns.

Human relations skills interact even more directly and clearly with leadership functions. A key to management is that tasks are performed not just by the manager but by and through the efforts of other people. Motivating, influencing, and supporting others' behaviors require strong interpersonal competency, whether the object of the leadership activity is a supervisee or a local citizen, an individual staff member or a group participating in a problem-solving meeting.

Finally, human relations skills affect the human service manager's ability to carry out evaluation processes. Not surprisingly, many workers find evaluation threatening. Yet the active participation of all agency employees, at least in data gathering, is necessary to carrying out the evaluation function. If evaluations are to be accurate and if their results are really going to be used as a basis for managerial decisions, cooperative efforts are essential.

The skill of working effectively with individuals and groups runs through the performance of every managerial function, and human service professionals may well find their backgrounds more useful than expected. Professional training can also enhance the development of skills in individual or joint decision making.

DECISION-MAKING SKILLS

Management is, in a very basic sense, a process of making decisions. From deciding whether to spin off a new agency to choosing the location of a water cooler, from selecting a new staff member to considering alternate data forms, the manager is in the position of constantly choosing among alternatives. Deciding, along with communicating, is what a manager actually does with his or her time.

Decision making involves identifying and weighing alternate means for reaching desired ends. In human service settings, the selection of the best means for achieving an objective is often far from easy. Because of the high degree of uncertainty that will always be present in dealing with human needs, completely rational decision making is impossible. Basic values, desired goals, and the wishes of sometimes opposing factions need to be taken into account. In this context, decision-making skill requires sensitivity as much as rationality.

When carrying out the planning function, human service professionals need to decide what approaches to use in assessing needs, how to involve community members and other stakeholders in the goal-setting process, and what reasonable objectives for a program might be. These decisions actually precede

15

the real decision-making challenge: choosing the most effective combination of services to meet the specified objectives. No one administrator or service deliverer makes these decisions alone. Involvement in cooperative decision making, however, is, if anything, more complex than choosing alternatives on the basis of one person's judgment.

Budgeting is also a decision-making activity. Whether working alone or as a member of a planning group, the human service professional must help decide how resources are to be allocated. Especially in times of economic stress, each positive choice can bring with it the need to make a negative decision somewhere else. Choosing to fund one activity means choosing not to fund another.

The decisions that are made as part of designing programs and structuring the organization also have far-reaching implications. In organizing, the manager must weigh the benefits of varying methods of dividing tasks among individuals and departments. The choices made invariably have major effects on the behaviors and productivity of all members of the service delivery team.

In providing leadership for this team, the manager continues to choose among alternate interventions, methods, and targets for change. Each decision affects both the immediate situation and the life of the agency as a whole. Ultimately, evaluation completes the administrative cycle by measuring the effects of past decisions and laying the groundwork for new choices.

LEADERSHIP AND CHANGE MANAGEMENT: KEEPING THE ORGANIZATION RESPONSIVE AND VIBRANT

The managerial functions previously described need to be implemented in order for programs to be effectively maintained. Fortunately for human service managers, the practical, human skills that underlie managerial functions are closely allied with the skills of helping. Social work, counseling, and psychology degree programs, in particular, emphasize effective communication skills such as active listening, giving and receiving feedback, group dynamics and facilitation, and positive regard for all individuals. All these skills are important for managers as they design systems and lead staff in accomplishing organizational goals.

In an era of accountability and limited resources, human service professionals cannot afford the luxury of attending to their own customary activities in isolation from general agency goals and operations. Service providers must know how their activities relate to programs and how these programs, in turn, relate to agency and community priorities. Human service professionals, like everyone with a stake in an agency's continued existence, must be aware of managerial processes that enable them to function on a daily basis (how their check is paid, why they need to keep good client records, why evaluations need to occur). Conveying this information and helping staff come to appreciate its importance is a task requiring leadership.

As Figure 1.2 illustrates, leadership is the unifying factor for all management processes. Agency executives and, in fact, managers at all levels need to be leaders who help keep the organization and all staff focused on key organizational outcomes and processes necessary to get there; provide energy, confidence, and optimism regarding meeting the challenges facing human service organizations; and oversee the agency's constant evolution and change so that it remains responsive to community needs and concerns. In briefly revisiting Figure 1.1 on organizational purpose, both the technical and leadership functions of management can be seen. The manager addresses the technical system functions through overseeing organizational processes including planning, program and organization design, human resources management and supervision, financial management, and monitoring and evaluation. The manager addresses the social system by providing leadership and vision, articulating key values and ethical standards, ensuring a vibrant organizational culture and high quality of working life, and overseeing constant organizational learning and change.

Change management is a major responsibility for leaders. Chapter 2 will outline some of the powerful external forces affecting human service organizations, pointing out the need for ongoing adaptation and change. As will be seen in Chapter 11, nearly every viable contemporary leadership approach includes change management. Leaders are not always the drivers of change, however, and even when they desire change, they sometimes need expertise from an outside source. Organization development, business process reengineering, total quality management, and other change processes are increasingly being used in human service organizations, with both good and disappointing results. Finally, there are techniques for lower-level employees to identify change opportunities and make proposals for improving agency operations. Leadership and change management are the ways that organizational processes and systems are kept up-to-date and responsive so that the agency can be maximally effective and thrive in an increasingly challenging environment.

THE MULTICULTURAL ORGANIZATION

We cannot think of organizational excellence and vibrancy without attending to the vital issue of multiculturalism and diversity. At the center of change-focused leadership is the need to move the organization toward a true commitment in this arena. Effective practitioners across all of the helping professions now recognize that they must be sensitive to cultural differences between themselves and their clients. Less progress has been made, however, in recognizing that multicultural competence is not just an individual characteristic but also a vital organizational characteristic.

> Organizational entities that fail to successfully implement diversity into the very structures of their operations will fail to be relevant to their clients or consumers. In the mental health field, clinics and providers must begin to alter the nature of their service delivery systems to recognize cultural diversity. The development of culturally appropriate mental health delivery systems for a diverse population may require major changes in the very structure of the organization. (Sue & Constantine, 2005, p. 213)

17

The development of excellence in this area may involve a process along a continuum from a monocultural organization to a nondiscriminatory organization to a multicultural organization (Sue, 1995). In the United States, a *monocultural organization* would characterized by (1) exclusion, whether conscious or not, of people from oppressed populations, (2) structures and processes that maintain privileged positions for people from the dominant majority, (3) management based on the values of the dominant culture, and (4) an assumption that employees and clients should adhere to dominant values. A *nondiscriminatory organization* represents a step forward in cultural awareness, but lacks consistent organizational policies and practices to support it. Multiculturalism and diversity have not yet become true organizational priorities. As an organization moves toward becoming a *multicultural organization* it demonstrates a valuing of diversity and consistently engages in "envisioning, planning, and problem-solving activities that allow for equal access and opportunities" (Sue, 1995, p. 485).

> We define a multicultural organization as committed (action as well as words) to diverse representation throughout all levels, sensitive to maintaining an open, supportive, and responsive environment, working toward and purposefully including elements of diverse cultures in its ongoing operations, carefully monitoring organizational policies and practices for the goals of equal access and opportunity, and authentic in responding to changing policies and practices that block cultural diversity. (Sue & Constantine, 2005, p. 223)

According to Sue and Constantine, certain conditions must exist in order for an organization to become multicultural in outlook. These characteristics include the following:

- "Multicultural commitment must come from the very top levels." (p. 223)
- "Each organization should have a written policy, mission statement, or vision statement that frames the concepts of multiculturalism and diversity into a meaningful operational definition." (p. 223)
- "The organization should have a multicultural and diversity action plan." (p. 224)
- "Multicultural accountability must be built into the system." (p. 224)
- "The organization should create a superordinate or oversight team that is empowered to assess, develop, and monitor the organization's development with respect to the goals of multiculturalism." (p. 224)
- "Organizations must be unafraid to actively solicit feedback from employees related to issues of race, culture, gender, ethnicity, and sexual orientation." (p. 224)
- "Multicultural competence should be infused into evaluation criteria and used for hiring and promotion of employees." (p. 224)
- "Culturally sensitive organizations recognize that mentoring and support networks for employees of color are vital for their success." (p. 224)
- "Active coalition building and networking among minorities and women, for example, should be valued." (p. 224)

• "The organization must be committed to a systematic and long-term plan to educate the entire workforce concerning diversity issues." (p. 224)

Clearly, the kinds of values, commitments, and processes that lead toward the creation of a multicultural organization are also the characteristics of excellence in all organizational endeavors.

SUMMARY

Human service organizations exist to accomplish socially desirable purposes. Good management is an essential element in making agencies able to accomplish desired goals. This chapter has reviewed the management processes that are essential to organizational effectiveness. The chapters that follow will address these areas in greater detail. Chapter 2 will review the uniqueness of human service organizations and factors in the environment that need attention. Some methods for managing the environment will be described.

Chapter 3 will show how strategic planning can be used to respond to the environment. Chapters 4 through 10 will discuss how to design programs based on plans and then how to staff, fund, monitor, and evaluate them. Chapter 11 will focus on leading and changing organizations, and Chapter 12 will offer perspectives on how today's manager of human service programs can rise to the challenge of attaining organizational excellence.

DISCUSSION QUESTIONS

1. What do you perceive as the main differences between managing a human service organization and managing a business? Would the same skills, attitudes, and body of knowledge be appropriate for each?
2. Think about a human service organization with which you are familiar. Is it well man-

aged? How could its effectiveness be improved? Which managerial functions are being performed most effectively?
3. What skills would you need to develop to manage a human service program?

GROUP EXERCISE

Work in groups of six to eight people. Brainstorm as many answers as you can generate to the question "What are the characteristics of an effective professional helper?" Be sure to write down any ideas that anyone in the group suggests.

After completing this list, use a brainstorming approach again, this time to answer the question "What are the characteristics of an effective human service manager?"

Compare the two lists, discussing the following questions:

1. How great are the differences between effective helpers and good managers?
2. To what degree are our ideas about human service managers affected by our own stereotypes of business managers?

Case 1 | TRANSITIONS INTO MANAGEMENT

Review the situations of the individuals profiled at the beginning of this chapter. Choose one with which you can identify in some way and answer these questions from that person's perspective.

1. What prospective changes in role are facing this person?

2. If you were in this situation, what factors would you consider in assessing your career goals and the kinds of activities you would like to do at work?

3. If you moved further into management, what additional skills and training would you need?

REFERENCES

Asamoah, Y. (1995). Managing the new multicultural workforce. In L. Ginsberg & P. Keys (Eds.), *New management in human services* (2nd ed., pp. 115–127). Washington, DC: NASW Press.

Bailey, D. (1995). Management: Diverse workplaces. In R. Edwards (Ed.), *Encyclopedia of social work* (19th ed., pp. 1659–1663). Washington, DC: NASW Press.

Harvey, C. (1998). Defining excellence in human service organizations. *Administration in Social Work, 22*(1), 33–45.

Healy, L., Havens, C., & Pine, B. (1995). Women and social work management. In L. Ginsberg & P. Keys (Eds.), *New management in human services* (2nd ed., pp. 128–150). Washington, DC: NASW Press.

Kretzmann, J., & McKnight, J. (1996). Assets-based community development. *National Civic Review, 85*(4), 23–27.

Rapp, C., & Poertner, J. (1992). *Social administration: A client-centered approach*. New York: Longman.

Senge, P. (1990). *The fifth discipline*. New York: Doubleday.

Shulman, L. (1993). *Interactional supervision*. Washington, DC: NASW Press.

Sue, D. W. (1995). Multicultural organizational development. In J. G. Ponterotto, J. M. Cases, L. A. Suzuki, & C. M. Alexander (Eds.), *Handbook of multicultural counseling* (pp. 474–492). Thousand Oaks, CA: Sage.

Sue, D. W., & Constantine, M. G. (2005). Effective multicultural consultation and organizational development. In M. G. Constantine & D. W. Sue (Eds.), *Strategies for building multicultural competence in mental health and educational settings* (pp. 212–226). New York: Wiley.

Taylor, J., & Felten, D. (1993). *Performance by design: Sociotechnical systems in North America*. Upper Saddle River, NJ: Prentice Hall.

4 CHAPTER | ORGANIZATIONAL THEORY FOR HUMAN SERVICE ORGANIZATIONS

CHAPTER OUTLINE

Classical Theories

Bureaucracy

Scientific Management

Universal Management Principles

Classical Theories in Today's Human Service Organizations

Human Relations Approaches

The Human Resources Model

Open Systems Theory

Contemporary Developments

Professional Bureaucracies

Community-Based Organizations and Feminist Organizations

Japanese Management

Total Quality Management

The Excellence Movement

Business Process Reengineering

Employee Involvement and the Quality of Working Life

Reinventing Government

Learning Organizations

Contingency Theories

Summary

Discussion Questions

Case 4: The Community Career Center

References

Kurt Lewin, one of the great thinkers in the field of organizational behavior, said, "There's nothing so practical as a good theory" (Weisbord, 1987, p. 70). We all have theories about how things work and which variables affect other variables. Some are ones we have been taught (behaviorism, psychoanalysis, family systems theory); others guide our behavior although they have not been clearly articulated (for example, which intervention will work at a given time with a given client). This chapter is intended to provide a core of knowledge of organizational theories currently being articulated and used, so that a manager and those working with managers can consciously and thoughtfully choose an appropriate theory to enhance their effectiveness in an organizational context. Organizational theories have changed over time, so this chapter begins with a historical overview going back over the past century.

Few human service workers maintain clear awareness of the practical differences dividing organizational theorists. Although all thinkers in the field of organizational theory seek the "best" answers to the basic questions, they seldom agree about what those best answers really are. The designers of an organization are faced with a myriad of choices. They can build structures that are highly centralized and specialized or systems based on widespread decision-making responsibility and participation. They can departmentalize the organization's activities by joining all the people who perform a specific function, or they can build teams of people with differing but complementary skills. They can use traditional, hierarchical designs or experiment with task forces, committees, or even leaderless groups. The organization's form has major implications for the way its functions will be performed.

CLASSICAL THEORIES

Three prominent classical theories of organization originated in the nineteenth century. Sociologist Max Weber articulated theoretical principles of the ideal bureaucracy. Industrial engineer Frederick Taylor developed scientific management guidelines for the "best way" to supervise workers in a factory. Henri Fayol developed a set of management principles that are still influential today.

BUREAUCRACY

The earliest major thinker to formulate the concept of an ideal organization was Max Weber, who saw the "rational legal bureaucracy" as the efficient organization in its pure form (Gerth & Mills, 1958). Weber's ideal structure included high degrees of specialization and impersonality, authority based on comprehensive rules rather than on social relationships, clear and centralized hierarchies of authority and responsibility, prescribed systems of rules and procedures, hiring and promotion based solely on technical ability, and extensive use of written documentation.

Weber saw this pure system as a historical trend that would meet the needs posed by the increasing size of organizations and at the same time replace

22

unfairness and uncertainty with rationality and clarity. Perrow (1986) summarizes the key elements of the rational legal bureaucracy this way:

1. Equal treatment for all employees.
2. Reliance on expertise, skills, and experience relevant to the position.
3. No extra organizational prerogatives of the position; that is, the position is seen as belonging to the organization, not the person. The employee cannot use it for personal ends.
4. Specific standards of work and output.
5. Extensive record keeping dealing with the work and output.
6. Establishment and enforcement of rules and regulations that serve the interests of the organization.
7. Recognition that rules and regulations bind managers as well as employees; thus, employees can hold management to the terms of the employment contract. (p. 3)

Speed, precision, and reduction of friction were associated with the ideal bureaucracy because in this organization everyone would have a clear awareness of both his or her and others' functions. All aspects of the organization's work would be regulated. The repetitiveness of the work would bring with it both steadiness and high quality. Personal enmity and constant questioning would be replaced by rationality and regularity.

One of the most common criticisms of an organization, unit, procedure, or manager is that it or he or she is "too bureaucratic." On the other hand, Perrow (1986) asserts that "many of the 'sins' of bureaucracy really reveal the failure to bureaucratize sufficiently" (p. 5). Other complaints regarding a bureaucracy are that a person (usually a manager) is not qualified or that someone is receiving preferential treatment—both violations of the principles of bureaucracy. Clearly, one of the failures of modern human service organizations, particularly public sector ones, is that they have sometimes enthusiastically and single-mindedly misapplied bureaucratic thinking, and even Weber was "extremely critical of the way bureaucracy destroys spontaneity" (Gortner, Mahler, & Nicholson, 1997, p. 5).

Ultimately, most would admit that bureaucracy, as it was first articulated by Weber, might provide some useful principles. It is also true that bureaucracy alone is insufficient to fully guide modern managerial behavior, and the subsequent movements discussed later, starting with the human relations movement, do not replace bureaucracy but add to it. Bureaucratic thinking provides a foundation for personnel practices that many workers appreciate: clear job roles and performance expectations, fair treatment, and due process; but later models would need to add principles recognizing that individuals and situations also must be addressed with appreciation for their differences.

Although Weber's approach was philosophical, the ideals of clearly defined objectives, specialization, hierarchical chains of command, and responsibility commensurate with authority are also basic to the thinking of early management scientists such as Taylor (1911) and practitioners such as Fayol (1949). Taylor in particular has been vilified as much as bureaucracy has, but he also provided principles that are still useful.

SCIENTIFIC MANAGEMENT

Frederick Taylor, the founder of the scientific management school of organizational theory, focused on the assembly line: the core work processes of the organization. As an industrial engineer, Taylor mainly consulted in the steel industry at the turn of the twentieth century. He believed that engineers could study a work process such as loading steel onto railway cars and determine the "one best method" for the task to be done. Workers were then trained on exactly how to do their job and repeated the same task over and over through their shift. He used time and motion studies to observe workers and identify wasteful steps or movements.

Perhaps his best-known quote describes job requirements for one who loads pig iron (a ninety-two-pound piece of steel): "One of the very first requirements for a man who is fit to handle pig-iron . . . is that he shall be so stupid . . . that he more nearly resembles in his mental make-up the ox than any other type" (1912 hearings, cited in Sashkin, 1981, p. 208). "Taylorism" has come to refer to managers who assume their employees are stupid and need to be told what to do in excruciating detail, assuming that the manager is always right. In fact, Taylor was a complex person who believed that bosses should be "servants of the workmen" (Weisbord, 1987, p. 34) and that workers should share in the profits of the organization.

Taylor's main legacies today are work analysis methods used by industrial engineers (sometimes in human service settings) and profit-sharing plans for workers in industry. As was the case with bureaucracy, some principles such as scientifically analyzing the work to be performed and rewarding workers based on their performance are valuable and can be seen today in the quality movement and organizational reward systems.

UNIVERSAL MANAGEMENT PRINCIPLES

The final theorist of the classical school is Henri Fayol, a French contemporary of Weber and Taylor whose views became known as the universal principles school. He conceptualized the five basic functions of management (planning, organizing, commanding, coordinating, and controlling) and developed a set of principles for the design of an organization (Bowditch & Buono, 2005, pp. 8–9):

1. Division of work—Specialization of tasks and control of the number of people under each worker or manager improves effectiveness and efficiency.
2. Authority and responsibility—The person in authority has the right to give orders and the power to obtain obedience; responsibility emerges directly from authority.
3. Unity of command—No person should have more than one boss.
4. Remuneration—Pay should be fair and satisfactory to the employer and employee; no one should be under- or over-rewarded.
5. Esprit de corps—Morale and good feelings about the organization are enhanced by effective face-to-face communication and group cohesiveness.

Fayol also talked about the *gangplank,* a figurative bridge that enabled individuals at the same level but in different units or departments to talk directly to each other rather than using the chain of command (Sashkin, 1981). The term *gangplank* is, of course, pejorative in current language usage, but the concept of making connections across units or departments is valued today, possibly more than it ever has before. Effective managers are aware that having separate, unconnected *units* for each department bodes poorly for organizational efficiency and effectiveness.

Classical Theories in Today's Human Service Organizations

With classical management theories still prevalent in so many settings, we need to ask how relevant or useful they are for human service programs and agencies. A human service agency designed on the basis of classical principles would be organized so that all employees, including professionals, paraprofessionals, and clerical workers, would perform regular, specialized tasks. A counselor assigned to perform individual counseling with adolescents might spend all of his or her time in this activity, while other specialists might conduct group sessions or work with parents. Although the degree of specialization would depend on the agency's size and resources, each task would be related to the basic goals of the program as a whole. The activities to be performed in the interests of meeting these goals would have been identified first, and then competent individuals would have been selected and trained to carry them out. It would be understood that the resources and jobs involved in the program would belong not to individuals but to the agency, with replacement of individual workers being possible without disrupting the flow of work. (Agency activities would not change, for example, because a behaviorist was replaced by an Adlerian or because a social worker was replaced by a psychologist.) Each worker would report to one supervisor or director, who would have the authority and responsibility to carry out policies chosen by the ultimate authority (in the case of a human service agency, the ultimate authority is usually delegated to an executive director by a board of directors). Each human service professional—like every other worker—would understand the precise limits of his or her function. All similar clients would receive similar services.

The major contribution that classical theories offer to human service programs is in the area of unity of effort, with the idea that all of an organization's activities should relate to its general goals. Human service organizations could benefit from increased rationality in the planning process because one of the weaknesses of human service programs has been the tendency of professionals to perform the functions that are comfortable for them rather than those that can best meet the client-oriented goals of the agency or institution. The idea that a program or agency should have a clearly defined set of objectives that should be met through the coordinated efforts of all workers is one that could enhance the efficiency and effectiveness of helping professionals. Even the bureaucratic ideal of "impersonality" could have something to offer because, as Perrow (1986) points out, it involves the purging of "particularism" and discrimination or favoritism in hiring and service delivery.

25

The strengths of the classical approach are counteracted by its weaknesses, at least in human service programs. The major problems in applying classical management principles to the helping services lie in the insistence on specialization and centralized hierarchies of authority. Human service professionals tend to see themselves as having responsibility not just to their agencies or institutions but to their clients and professional colleagues as well. They are not easily able to conform to a system that expects them to obey orders that may conflict with their professional standards or their views of their clients' best interests. The use of very specialized, routine work patterns may be of little value in dealing with humans and their unique problems. The worker who gains a "habitual and virtuoso-like mastery" of his or her subject may overlook the differing needs of individuals being served, with the result that agency rules gain in ascendancy while consumer rights are lost.

Human service agencies are beginning to come to grips with the fact that creative approaches are needed to deal with the problem of increasing client needs coinciding with decreasing agency resources. Unfortunately, what bureaucracies may offer in terms of rationality is lost in terms of creativity. Some of these weaknesses are addressed by the proponents of the human relations approach.

HUMAN RELATIONS APPROACHES

The origins of the human relations approach to organization are usually traced to Elton Mayo. Mayo and his colleagues were involved in Western Electric's Hawthorne plant experiments in the 1920s and 1930s. These studies were undertaken to determine whether changes in the physical work environment affected worker productivity. In essence, they were designed to test some of the postulates of scientific management, specifically those having to do with the effects of illumination, fatigue, and production quotas on worker performance. The underlying purpose of the Hawthorne studies was to find means of increasing organizational efficiency. Small experimental and control groups of workers were identified and placed in separate rooms, where their work was closely observed and recorded by members of the research team. Environmental conditions for the experimental group were altered in both a positive and a negative direction; that is, the lights were turned up and down, rest periods were increased and decreased, and quotas were raised and lowered. Yet the group's productivity continued to increase steadily until it leveled off at a rate unaffected by environmental manipulations (Perrow, 1986).

Finding little support for the hypothesis that variations in environmental conditions (except for the extremely negative, such as almost total darkness) affect productivity, the researchers attributed major experimental results to social phenomena theretofore given slight importance by theorists. Mayo's conclusions included the following (Accel-Team, 2005a):

- Work is a group activity.
- The social world of the adult is primarily patterned about work activity.

- The need for recognition, security and sense of belonging is more important in determining a worker's morale and productivity than the physical conditions under which he works.
- A complaint is not necessarily an objective recital of facts; it is commonly a symptom manifesting disturbance of an individual's status position.
- The worker is a person whose attitudes and effectiveness are conditioned by social demands from both inside and outside the work plant.
- Informal groups within the workplace exercise strong social controls over the work habits and attitudes of the individual worker.
- Group collaboration does not occur by accident; it must be planned and developed. If group collaboration is achieved, the human relations within a work plant may reach a cohesion which resists disruption (that might otherwise be brought about through technological change).

At least two of these factors continue to have an impact on today's organizational practices: (a) the existence and influence of the informal group within the formal organization and (b) what later became known as the "Hawthorne effect." Both of these findings have implications for today's human service manager. The first has to do with issues of control; the second, with coordination—two important elements of organizational structure.

With respect to the informal group, the Hawthorne researchers found that the relationships formed among the members of the test groups appeared to meet certain social and psychological needs for affiliation that in turn led to enhanced group productivity. Moreover, findings indicated that informal group members established their own production rates based on their collective perception of survival within the organization rather than on quotas imposed by management. That is, the informal group determined at what point under-productivity might lead to being fired and over-productivity might lead to being laid off. Fortunately, and perhaps coincidentally, the Hawthorne subjects established a production rate that was within their managers' zone of acceptance (Perrow, 1986).

The Hawthorne experiments served more to illuminate the importance of the human element in organizational life than to demonstrate the importance of illumination on organizational productivity. Dimensions of worker motivation beyond fear and greed were introduced as valid managerial areas of concern and study.

The human relations approach to organization assumes that the bureaucratic view of human beings is too narrow to be useful in real-life organizations, and it has added immeasurably to views of organizational behavior and management practice. Nevertheless, the human relations school as developed following the Hawthorne studies was later seen to be incomplete as well. This conclusion required further thinking about how to address the human dimension to make organizations more effective.

Before we leave the human relations school, we will visit yet another contemporary of both the classical theorists and the Hawthorne experimenters. Mary Parker Follett was a hugely influential consultant to industry until her death in 1933 and subsequently in her writings (Graham, 1995). Of interest to human service managers, Follett had a twenty-five-year career as a social work manager in Boston before becoming famous as a speaker and writer focusing on the business sector (Syers, 1995, p. 2585). Her thinking predated and influenced such current concepts as participatory management and empowerment, total quality management, conflict management, and leadership (Selber & Austin, 1997). Some of these concepts will be discussed later, but one of her insights is particularly relevant to the transition from the human relations movement begun in the 1920s to a more advanced view articulated by writers including Argyris, McGregor, and Likert.

According to Child (1995), the human relations approach articulated by Mayo and others in fact supported the classical notion of managerial control, whereas Follett believed in substantive worker participation in decision making. In his words, the human relations view "ascribed a privileged rationality to managers that legitimated their authority and was naturally attractive to members of the management movement working on their behalf" (p. 88). The later developments in the human relations school are, in fact, substantively different from the earlier version, and this distinction was made by Miles (1965, 1975) as he assessed different types of employee participation in decision making. He defined his approach as the human resources model, which implied more fully using the skills and talents of workers than the human relations model of the Hawthorne studies, which has been derisively referred to as "cow sociology": keep the workers contented/happy and they will produce more milk/work.

THE HUMAN RESOURCES MODEL

An early humanistic psychologist, Argyris (1957) pointed out that workers are motivated by many factors other than economics, including desires for growth and independence. To Argyris, the organizational forms mandated by the classical theorists make for immature, dependent, and passive employees with little control over their work and thwart more mature employees capable of autonomy and independence. The purpose of the human resources approach is to develop organizational forms that build on the worker's strength and motivation.

McGregor (1960) distinguished between managers adhering to Theory X and those adhering to Theory Y. He did not say that either of these theories is correct. He did say that each is based on assumptions that, if recognized, would have major implications for organizing activities.

McGregor's Theory X manager assumes that people dislike work, lack interest in organizational objectives, and want to avoid responsibility. The natural result of this situation is that managers must base their organizations on the need to control; to supervise closely; and to use reward, punishment, and active persuasion to force employees to do their jobs. In contrast, the manager who adheres to Theory Y assumes that people enjoy working, desire responsibility, have innate capacities for creativity, and have the potential to work toward organizational objectives with a minimum of direction. The implication of these assumptions is that work can be organized in such a way that personnel at all levels have the opportunity to do creative, self-directed, and responsible jobs.

The organizational implications of McGregor's model are clear. Theory X managers would use high degrees of specialization, clear lines of authority, narrow spans of control, and centralized decision making. Theory Y managers would use less specialization, less control, and more delegation of decision making and responsibility. The organization would be decentralized so that workers' natural creativity could be channeled effectively.

Likert (1967) examined a number of specific organizational variables, including leadership, motivation, communication, decision making, goal setting, and control. He divided organizations into four basic types, based on how they deal with these organizational variables: System 1 (exploitive authoritative), System 2 (benevolent authoritative), System 3 (consultative), and System 4 (participative group). Likert's System 1 organizations are characterized by leaders who distrust their subordinates, decision-making processes that are concentrated at the top of the organizational hierarchy, and communication that is almost exclusively downward, from supervisor to supervisees. Control and power are centralized in top management so that others feel little concern for the organization's overall goals. System 2 organizations also centralize power in the hands of the few at the top of the hierarchy but add an increased degree of communication. More trust is placed in subordinates, but it is condescending in nature. System 3 increases communication; employees have the opportunity to give input, although all major decisions are still made at the top of the management hierarchy. System 4, the opposite of System 1, is characterized by leaders who have complete confidence in workers, motivation that is based on responsibility and participation as well as on economic rewards, communication among all organization members, extensive interaction, decentralized decision making, wide acceptance of organizational goals, and widespread responsibility for control.

Likert (1967, p. 46) said that most managers recognize System 4 as theoretically superior to the others. He pointed out that if clear plans, high goals, and technical competence are present in an organization, System 4 will be superior. The key to its superiority lies in a structure based on group decision making and on the relationship of each group in an organization to every other group through common members or linking pins.

How would an organization based on the thinking of Mayo, Follett, Argyris, McGregor, and Likert differ from a bureaucratic agency? If a human service program were organized in accordance with a human relations or human resources approach, it would be characterized by greater freedom of action, both for human service professionals and for their coworkers. Instead of departmentalizing the agency by function, the organization might divide work according to purpose or population being served. An interdisciplinary task force, including various helping professionals, paraprofessionals, community

29

members, and consumers, might work together to solve a specific problem. Such a group might design a program to improve the agency's services to court-referred juveniles or troubled families. It might provide outreach services to displaced homemakers or school-age drug users. It might educate the community concerning mental health or stress management.

The task force itself might be permanent or ad hoc, but this organizational structure would allow each person to participate actively in planning and decision making while decreasing the prevalence of routine, specialized activities. Less attention would be directed toward authority and control, and greater emphasis would be placed on the flow of information from person to person and group to group. In the case of a large agency, people would identify with their own projects and feel responsible for their success. In the case of a small agency or a program within a larger institution, all staff members would participate in setting objectives and choosing evaluation methods for the program as a whole. Although a hierarchy of authority might exist, decision-making powers would not be limited to those at the highest levels, and the boundaries between jobs and specializations would not be clear-cut. Structure would be seen as a changing force rather than a constant factor.

A strength of the human resources school for human service agencies is its consistency with the approach of helping professionals. Human service workers tend to favor increasing self-responsibility and options for their clients, and they generally prefer that their supervisors give them high levels of autonomy, as the human resources school prescribes.

The human resources–based organization also has a greater allowance for change than does the bureaucratic structure. Although bureaucracies are efficient for dealing with routine tasks, they do not allow for the creative responses to change that a more fluid environment can make. The human service field needs new approaches to help clients deal with a continually changing world. Professionals who have the opportunity to create and the freedom to innovate might provide better service than their highly specialized colleagues.

Of course, the human resources theories do not provide easy answers. Creating an organization based on concepts of democracy and independence is, if anything, a more complex task than developing a more traditional structure. Although people might have innate capacities for growth and creativity, they have not necessarily had the chance to develop these capacities in schools and work settings that still tend toward Theory X. The Theory Y manager must carefully create structures that can encourage workers to learn how to function without close supervision and at the same time provide effective training and leadership.

A final note is that human service organizations are often closely related to larger systems, and a structure that differs greatly from those used by others is often misunderstood. A System 4 counseling department, for example, within a System 1 school or a System 4 community agency attempting to deal with a System 1 city government would face conflicts that might seem surprising.

OPEN SYSTEMS THEORY

Systems can be thought of as sets of elements that interact with one another so that a change in any one of those elements brings about a corresponding alteration in other elements. Open systems take in and export energy through interfaces with the environment so that units within the system are also affected by changes in other systems. Open systems theorists recognize that rationality within organizations is limited by both internal factors, such as organization members' characteristics, and external factors, such as changes in the supply of available people and materials.

What are the characteristics of a system? As defined by Accel-Team (2005b, p. 6):

- A system is defined by its properties.
- A system is a physical and/or conceptual entity composed of interrelated and interacting parts existing in an environment with which it may also interact.
- The system has a preferred state.
- The parts of the system may in turn be systems themselves.

Theoretically, there could be *closed systems* that do not interact with their environments. In fact, however, all systems are affected by their environments. An *open system* has a two-way interaction with the environment, affecting the environment and being affected by it in return. Any organization, as a system, would fall somewhere on the continuum between a closed and an open system.

The fact that the system has a preferred state means that it tries to maintain itself in a stable, steady state, or *homeostasis*. The system reacts to change by making adaptations in ways that bring it back to its homeostasis without changing its essential character. Systems vary in their ability to carry out these adaptations.

An adaptive system is one that is capable of responding to changes in the condition of the environment or to contingencies imposed by the environment. A non-adaptive system does not react to its environment.

- A perfectly adaptive system can respond to any change or contingency in the environment.
- All systems lie somewhere between non-adaptive and perfectly adaptive systems.
- In order to continue existing, any open system in a dynamic environment must adapt. (Accel-Team, 2005b, p. 8)

Managers who view their organizations from the systems perspective tend to see the organization more as a process than as a structure. They know that structural changes both affect and are affected by changes in all the other components of the organization. They know, too, that the goals and activities they choose will be influenced by environmental factors that are often beyond their control.

The ideas offered by systems theory might well be more important to human service agencies than to private-sector firms because environmental

31

effects on both the program as a whole and individual clients must be considered. Human service professionals using these ideas would develop structures indicating the relationships between the agency and other systems as well as those within the agency. Methods of coordination with community groups, funding sources, government agencies, other helping agencies, educational institutions, professional organizations, and a variety of other systems would need to be identified. In addition, organizational strategies would take into account the progress of individual clients through the system. Methods would be developed for linking clients with various services, following up on clients as they move into other systems, and communicating with referring agencies as new clients are accepted. These methods would be built into the organizational structure, with communication to outside agencies planned as carefully as communication within the program itself.

A major strength of the systems approach is the encouragement it gives to human service professionals to think of themselves as part of a network that, as a totality, can serve the individual client in a coordinated way. This does not mean that human service administrators should allow their programs to be buffeted about by external systems, all making conflicting demands. The other organizational approaches, including the classical management approach, provide some benefits as well, for they can help agencies in their attempts to clarify basic program goals and to find ways to develop unity of effort in reaching those goals.

Most of the organizational theories and principles that have emerged over the last half-century operate under the assumption that all formal organizations are in fact open systems that respond to the environments around them. Organizations have to devise new ways of addressing emerging community needs and goals, competition from other organizations, and a workforce with changing expectations regarding the quality of working life.

CONTEMPORARY DEVELOPMENTS

Since the last major historical period of organizational theory in the 1960s, new practice models and major movements have proliferated, including the quality movement, the excellence movement, and, in the human services, the advent of community-based organizations. While it may seem odd to refer to the past half-century as "contemporary," these trends are in fact still considered to be recent and continue to evolve as they are applied in different ways in different settings. All have relevance for human service organizations.

PROFESSIONAL BUREAUCRACIES

Two particular characteristics of bureaucracy, centralization ("the degree to which decision making authority is confined to the top echelons of the bureau or assigned to the lower echelon offices and officials" [Gortner et al., 1997, p. 95]) and formalization ("the extent to which expectations concerning job activities are standardized and explicit" [Bowditch & Buono, 2005, p. 270]), have caused problems in organizations doing nonroutine work, including human service organizations. Professional employees want decision making to be decentralized and formal rules to be lessened, giving them more autonomy. Employees who have professional training can make all the decisions covered by their professional codes, but they do not necessarily take agency goals, or even changing client needs, into account. On the other hand, a centralized bureaucracy cannot be successfully implemented because the presence of a large number of professionals confounds the hierarchy and eliminates unquestioning subservience to agency-wide objectives.

An adaptation of bureaucracy has emerged to deal with these problems: the "professional bureaucracy" (Mintzberg, 1979, 1992). Like the traditional bureaucracy, this type of organization depends on the regularity of the tasks to be performed, standardization, and stability. The tasks to be performed in the professional bureaucracy, however, are too technical and complex to be dictated by managers. Instead, authority is based on professional expertise, so the regularity of the bureaucracy is combined with a high degree of decentralization. Each professional worker controls his or her own technology in terms of professional standards and training, even though some of the skills used may be repetitive. "The professional bureaucracy emphasizes authority of a professional nature—the power of expertise":

> Change in the professional bureaucracy does not sweep in from new administrators taking office to announce major reforms. Rather, change seeps in by the slow process of changing the Professionals: changing who can enter the profession, what they learn in its professional schools (norms as well as skills and knowledge), and thereafter how willing they are to upgrade their skills. (12manage, 2005, p. 2)

In a professional bureaucracy, conflict can occur between professional judgments and agency policies, especially in a public-sector agency with many rules, some of which may originate outside the organization and are based on federal or state laws and regulations. As a principle of organization design, professionals in such settings sometimes need to advocate for the use of decision-making models such as the human resources approach to enable them to use their professional judgment with individual cases. A complication of this model occurs when multiple professions operate within the same organization, such as a hospital, where there may be disagreements among various professionals involved with a case.

COMMUNITY-BASED ORGANIZATIONS AND FEMINIST ORGANIZATIONS

Another reaction to bureaucracies emerged in the human service field in the 1960s with the advent of small, nonbureaucratic, not-for-profit organizations originally known as "street" or "alternative" agencies (Perlmutter, 1988). These agencies developed as an alternative to traditional bureaucracies, which were seen as ignoring or oppressing particular people in need, such as runaways and drug addicts. They were usually started by small groups of committed individuals who ran their programs on very small budgets, initially with little or no government funding and often using donated facilities, furniture, and equipment. According to Perlmutter (1995, pp. 204–205), these programs typically had the following characteristics:

- They were deeply committed to social change.
- They were reluctant to acknowledge the reality and legitimacy of formal authority and power.
- They were designed to meet the needs of special populations not being serviced by existing agencies.
- Their services were often exploratory or innovative.
- Staff were deeply committed ideologically to clients, were closely identified with them, or were former clients.
- Small size of the agency was valued.
- Agencies were usually in a marginal economic position.

Alternative agency staff believed that runaways and substance abusers, for example, should not be treated as criminals but should be given appropriate social services. They ran their agencies using democratic or consensus decision making, eschewing an all-powerful director.

Over the course of the 1970s, these programs grew, often by becoming more "mainstream" and acquiring government funding, or in some cases remained small and true to their original philosophies, or died. During this period, Holleb and Abrams (1975) suggested that such programs would eventually become bureaucratic, like the agencies they originally reacted against, or would be able to hold onto their original values and principles, a stage they called "consensual democracy." This would involve developing organizational forms in line with these values while somehow accommodating the inevitabilities of growth and becoming more formalized in operations.

Today, it is sometimes hard to see these philosophical origins of community-based organizations with multimillion-dollar budgets, professional staffs, and mainstream facilities. While some agencies are comfortable with their status as more traditional service providers, others work hard to maintain what is special about their original values while adapting to the world of purchase-of-service contracting. Feminist organizations in fields such as domestic violence have demonstrated some success at maintaining their original ideologies (Gilson, 1997).

Perlmutter (1995) has suggested that administrators of such programs who want to avoid becoming traditional and bureaucratic need to hold firmly to their values and ideology and be comfortable with risk taking, difference and diversity, and periods of economic uncertainty. She adds that such organizations need to be constantly vigilant, focusing on their missions, being alert to environmental challenges, and attending to fund-raising. Administrators need to use nonauthoritarian management styles, develop effective interpersonal skills, and be sensitive to staff issues including possible burnout. Similar practice principles are advocated by those practicing progressive social work (Bombyk, 1995).

Japanese Management

By now many Americans are familiar with the story of the advent of the quality movement, traced to the importation from Japan of quality circles in the 1980s as the United States had to recognize the dominance of Japan in manufacturing high-quality products at low cost. Ironically, the methods that changed Japan's reputation as a manufacturer of cheap goods to that of a world leader came originally from America, largely through statistician W. E. Deming and others who provided training to Japanese industry after World War II (Schmidt & Finnegan, 1992). With the subsequent problems in the Japanese economy becoming public in the 1990s, many began to question the value of Japanese management methods. Regardless of the state of the Japanese economy, the principles of quality that became popular there are still relevant and important in American organizations, including the human services. Ouchi's (1982) Theory Z provided a good summary of this movement into the early 1980s.

Ouchi developed Theory Z through his study of Japanese corporations. His findings were that Japanese organizations were characterized by lifetime employment, slow evaluation and promotion, nonspecialized career paths, collective decision-making styles, collective responsibility, and an integration of work and social lives. In the increasingly global economy of the 1990s, many of these principles evolved significantly; in fact, some of the weaknesses associated with these principles, such as the encouragement of workaholic behavior, have since become evident. Lifetime employment, never a reality for the majority of Japanese companies, became much less common in the economic crisis of the 1990s. The common policy of not laying off employees has changed radically recently, with increasing reports of companies "bullying" employees into quitting so that they will not have to be paid severance pay and retirement benefits (Mangier, 1999).

While the term *Theory Z* is rarely used today, its most valuable principles have been incorporated in other ways in many American organizations. Principles of Japanese management have been summarized for use in the human services by Keys (1995a), who studied their use in Japanese social welfare agencies. These include flexible job descriptions; informal decision-making processes to build consensus before formal decisions are made; training and team building to foster shared values, consensus, and high morale; job reassignment and rotation, in which staff have temporary assignments in other departments or agencies, to foster teamwork and collaboration; and total quality management.

Of these processes and principles, total quality management has received the most attention in American organizations. We will now look at how it has been applied in the human services in the United States.

Total Quality Management

In an organization using total quality management (TQM), "the organization's culture is defined by and supports the constant attainment of customer satisfaction through an integrated system of tools, techniques, and training"

(Sashkin & Kiser, cited in Keys, 1995b, p. 2019). The seven primary tenets of TQM have been summarized by Swiss (in Keys, 1995b) this way:

1. First and foremost, the customer is the ultimate determiner of quality.
2. Quality should be built into the product [or service] early in the production (upstream) rather than being added on at the end (downstream).
3. Preventing variability is the key to producing high quality.
4. Quality results from people working within systems, not individual efforts.
5. Quality requires continuous improvement of inputs and processes.
6. Quality improvement requires strong worker participation.
7. Quality requires total organizational commitment. (p. 2020)

Keys (1995b) notes that teams (cross-functional improvement teams, quality circles, and process improvement teams) are an "essential component of TQM" (p. 2021). Other basic TQM tools are used for data collection and analysis of work processes, including statistical process charts and flow charts, Pareto charts, and cause-effect diagrams. Another term that has become part of the process improvement vernacular is *benchmarking,* which involves surveys of other organizations to identify the best practices for accomplishing a particular procedure and setting these as standards (Ammons, 1998). TQM techniques are described in more detail by Hawkins and Gunther (1998) and Gummer and McCallion (1995).

THE EXCELLENCE MOVEMENT

With their publication of *In Search of Excellence,* Peters and Waterman (1982) called attention to the ingredients of successful megacorporations in our society. In almost evangelical tones, they summarize their studies of excelling organizations as follows:

> The findings from the excellent companies amount to an upbeat message. There is good news from America. Good management today is not resident only in Japan. But, more important, the good news comes from treating people decently and asking them to shine, and from producing things that work. Scale efficiencies give way to small units with turned-on people. Precisely planned R & D efforts aimed at big bang products are replaced by armies of dedicated champions. A numbing focus on cost gives way to an enhancing focus on quality. Hierarchy and three-piece suits give way to first names, shirt sleeves, hoopla, and project-based flexibility. Working according to fat rule books is replaced by everyone's contributing. (p. xxv)

Structure, Peters and Waterman conclude, is only "a small part of the total issue of management effectiveness" (p. 9). Among the several other variables identified by these authors in their examination of organizational achievement is "shared values," or organizational culture. This focus has been adopted by several other studies on organizational culture, including those by Cooke and Rousseau (1988), Schein (1992), and Trice and Beyer (1993). (Findings and implications from the "cultural school" of organizational theory are more fully discussed in Chapter 11, which deals with organizational change.)

The research of Peters and Waterman was criticized shortly after their book was published, as it was noted that some of the companies they profiled did not do well in subsequent years (Micklethwait & Wooldridge, 1997, pp. 14–15). However, their general principles have continued to be relevant, if not treated as universal prescriptions. These have been adapted to governmental organizations by Bryson (1995, p. 294):

Local Government Excellence Criteria	Peters and Waterman Criteria
Action orientation: quickly identify and fix problems	A bias for action
Listen to citizens and strive to meet their needs	Close to the customer
Encourage autonomy and entrepreneurship through innovation and risk taking	Autonomy and entrepreneurship
Employee orientation: trust and respect them	Productivity through people
Articulate and act based on values	Hands-on, value driven
Focus on the organization's unique mission, goals, and competence	Stick to the "knitting" (that is, do not provide services outside the organization's distinctive areas of competence)
Simplify structures	Simple form, lean staff
Maintain supportive and effective political relationships	Simultaneous loose-tight properties

There have also been some applications of excellence principles in human service agencies specifically (Harvey, 1998; National Assembly of National Voluntary Health and Social Welfare Organizations, 1989).

Peters and Waterman each published subsequent books, and Peters in particular has become even more evangelical in showcasing additional "excellent" organizations and leaders. Since he uses case studies and generally has not clearly outlined his research methods, it is difficult to isolate specifically the key success factors of the organizations that he profiles. The complexity and contradictions in his work have been profiled by Micklethwait and Wooldridge (1997), who give him premier "management guru" status. The greatest value of Peters and other "paradigm busters" may be not in the substance of their recommendations but the way they encourage managers to question their assumptions and try to do better.

BUSINESS PROCESS REENGINEERING

Quality improvement processes began to be applied at an organization-wide level with the advent of business process reengineering (BPR) (Hammer & Champy, 1993), also known as business process improvement. BPR has been defined as "a fundamental rethinking and radical redesign of business processes to achieve dramatic improvements in critical contemporary measures of performance such as cost, quality service, and speed" (Hammer & Champy, 1993, p. 32). Whereas TQM focuses on the line-level organizational processes, reengineering focuses on the whole organization, with particular attention to the "silo mentality" in which different functions operate in separate silos without communicating with each other, and on eliminating all organizational processes that do not add value to the product or service for the customer. It quickly became known as a rationale or excuse for downsizing (euphemistically known as "rightsizing") and other cost-cutting initiatives.

Managers and stockholders became so infatuated with these developments that a new term, corporate anorexia, entered the management vocabulary: organizations had cut so many staff that they no longer had the institutional memory and brain power to respond effectively to subsequent environmental changes. Rehiring began as the economy improved, although in many cases new hires were contract or temporary employees. Reengineering also received a more critical look at this time when studies showed that 70 to 85 percent of reengineering efforts failed (Zell, 1997, p. 23). In the scientific management tradition, BPR focused on the technical and rational aspects of the organization, ignoring everything that had been learned about human resources approaches. Micklethwait and Wooldridge (1997), who devote a whole chapter to BPR as the "fad in progress" in their critique of management gurus, document its weaknesses and failures, concluding that is does have appropriate, if limited, uses and that it is most effective when used in a "holistic" way, with attention to human factors and employee involvement. Useful design criteria that are based on reengineering principles and are relevant to human service organizations will be reviewed in the next chapter.

EMPLOYEE INVOLVEMENT AND THE QUALITY OF WORKING LIFE

Employee involvement as a management technology was based on human resources theories and the model of quality circles developed in Japan. It was refined and recontextualized through the quality of working life (QWL) movement, which reached prominence in the 1970s and is most fundamentally concerned with more fully involving subordinates in key organizational decisions. Its applications in the human services, most commonly referred to as participative decision making, will be covered in Chapter 7 as part of the supervision process. It is mentioned here at the organizational level because it has implications for the macrolevel design of the organization.

The QWL movement was important because it went beyond earlier conceptions of human relations and job satisfaction, on the one hand, and analytical approaches such as scientific management, on the other, by looking holistically at both technical processes such as how the work got done and social processes such as how decisions were made. According to Taylor and Felten (1993):

> Quality of working life is more than merely wages, hours, and working conditions; it is more than dignity and respect, social support, prospects for advancement, and

challenging work. Employees (management and nonmanagement alike) have an opportunity to experience higher QWL through (a) a sense of importance or relevance of their product to the larger community, (b) through the understanding of their place or direct role in creating the product, and (c) through the opportunity to become competent in dealing with those activities most central to the effective creation of the product. (p. 127)

In an old but still relevant overview, Walton (1975) groups QWL factors into eight areas: adequate and fair compensation, safe and healthy working conditions, immediate opportunity to use and develop human capacities (such as autonomy and multiple skills), opportunity for continued growth and security, social integration in the work organization (egalitarianism, freedom from prejudice), constitutionalism in the work organization, work and the total life space (a balanced role of work: time for family and leisure), and the social relevance of work life (the organization's social responsibility).

QWL principles align well with the expectations that typical professionals would have for human service work, but because of bureaucratic processes and other conditions, they are not always present. QWL "programs" were popular in the 1970s, but more recently QWL is used as a set of underlying principles for employee involvement to enhance organizational effectiveness, most prominently in sociotechnical systems design, which will be covered in Chapter 5 as a model for organization redesign. The concept is also used for assessing organizational conditions in need of change. This is often done using employee attitude surveys, an organizational change strategy reviewed in Chapter 12. QWL principles, as given here or as developed for a particular organization, can be very useful as design criteria for changing an organization's structure and processes.

REINVENTING GOVERNMENT

In a groundbreaking book, Osborne and Gaebler (1992) profile dynamic governmental organizations that exemplify a new "entrepreneurial spirit" in government bureaucracies. Reinvention is defined as "the fundamental transformation of public systems and organizations to create dramatic increases in their effectiveness, efficiency, adaptability, and capacity to innovate" (Osborne & Plastrik, 1997, p. 13). As summarized by Bryson (1995), Osborne and Gaebler suggest that governments should have the following qualities:

- Catalytic—They should focus on steering rather than rowing. Government should decide what should be done but does not have to do it itself.
- Community-owned—The programs that work best are the ones that are community owned, capacity building, and empowering rather than delivered by bureaucracies to clients.
- Competitive—Competition is to be preferred to monopoly provision of service since competition is more likely to lead to better, more innovative, and less expensive service.
- Mission-driven—Government should be animated by mission and vision rather than driven by rules.

39

- Results-oriented—Funding should be based on outcomes, not inputs.
- Customer-driven—Government should meet the needs of the customer and citizen, not the bureaucracy.
- Enterprising—Entrepreneurship and earning money should be rewarded more than spending money.
- Anticipatory—The focus of attention should be on preventing rather than curing problems.
- Decentralized—Participation and teamwork should be emphasized more than hierarchy.
- Market-oriented—Governments should think creatively about how to use markets to achieve public purposes. (p. 295)

Micklethwait and Wooldridge (1997), who earlier offered thoughtful criticism of reengineering, encourage government managers to be guarded in their adoption of management "fads" such as reinvention. They conclude, however, that "management theory has clearly brought more good than harm to the public sector" (p. 316) and suggest that managers take thoughtful reforms even further. As was the case for the study of excellent organizations, reinventing government principles should not be taken as models to apply exactly but as guidelines for creative thinking and selective adoption based on unique organizational circumstances.

LEARNING ORGANIZATIONS

In 1990, Peter Senge published *The Fifth Discipline: The Art and Practice of the Learning Organization*. It became a modern classic and was followed by two guidebooks (Senge et al., 1999; Senge et al., 1994) that describe how to create and nurture learning organizations. The five disciplines discussed by Senge are personal mastery (personal growth and learning), mental models (deeply held images about how the world works), shared vision (alignment of personal visions), team learning (using dialogue to address difficult issues), and systems thinking (a conceptual framework for observing patterns and seeing how to change them).

Becoming a learning organization in the sense described by Senge is a very difficult and time-consuming process that, if approached with energy and diligence, can be very rewarding. Reports of learning organization applications in the human services have been rare (Cohen & Austin, 1994; Kurtz, 1998), which perhaps indicates the difficulty of applying such principles. Learning organization concepts seem compatible with human service principles such as the use of teams and dialogue, and they represent opportunities for growth in human service organizations.

CONTINGENCY THEORIES

The preceding review of classic and current theories and models offers a rich menu from which to choose promising innovations for management practice. No one form of organization is appropriate for all types of settings. In fact, principles from many or all of the theories discussed here may be useful in a given human service organization. Several researchers have indicated that organizational technologies (tasks), environments, and even sizes affect strategy, which should help determine structure. Different organizations bring with them the need for different structures. Determination of the most efficient and productive type of structure in a given situation depends on the specific contingencies being faced.

The contingency theories—unlike the traditional, human relations, and human resources approaches—recognize that there is no "one best way" to structure all organizations. Rather, a number of "contingency" factors have differential effects on organizations and should be considered in designing structure.

Contingency theories are, in effect, systems theories in the sense that they recognize the effect of the organization's external environment on its internal structure. The contingency perspective, in other words, accounts for the importance of the interaction between the organization and the outside world— a world that provides it with the sanctions (legitimacy, societal acceptance, political support), energy (money, technological advances, human resources), and raw materials (microchips, steel, human beings) to meet its goals. Just as individuals are affected by their environment—its climatic fluctuations, the quality of its atmosphere—so are organizations subject to their environments. Adaptation to new environmental conditions is accomplished, as was reviewed in Chapter 3, through the design and implementation of new programs. Organizational adaptation at a larger scale is accomplished through designing or, more typically, redesigning the organization. This reflects Chandler's (1962) principle that structure follows strategy: once members of the organization decide where they want to go, the best structure and organizational processes are developed to enable the organization as a system to implement its programs and thrive in a complex environment.

The work of Lawrence and Lorsch (1967) provides particular insight into organizational needs in varying situations. Lawrence and Lorsch identify four organizational features that vary with the degree of environmental certainty: (1) reliance on formal rules and communication, (2) time horizon, (3) diffuse or concentrated goals, and (4) relationship- or task-oriented interpersonal styles. They stress that effective organizations have a good "fit" with their environment. An organization with a stable environment can use formal rules, a short time horizon, traditional communication channels, and task-oriented management. An organization with an unstable environment needs more points of contact with the external world so that changes can be recognized promptly. Such an organization also requires a longer time orientation and a more complex communication pattern. Formal rules and hierarchies would interfere with the needed information flow, so it would be inappropriate to rely on them.

Burns and Stalker (1994) distinguish between what they term mechanistic and organic forms of organization. The mechanistic form, comparable to the classical type of structure, depends on formal authority, specialization, and structured channels of communication. The organic form is highly flexible and informal, with communication channels based not on the hierarchical chain of command but on the need to solve immediate problems by consulting the person with the needed data. In studying a number of British firms, Burns and

41

Stalker found that the organic style seems most appropriate for firms such as electronics companies facing rapid technological change and the need to solve novel problems. The mechanistic form is productive for firms needing efficiency in dealing with very stable conditions.

The contingency theorists make clear that an effective organization can run the gamut from a traditional bureaucracy to a highly organic, constantly changing structure. Which structure is appropriate depends on the organization's needs. At its most basic level the contingency approach offers administrators a method for clarifying their ideas about organization.

If human service professionals were to use contingency theory to determine the best ways to structure the work of their programs or agencies, they would, as a first step, identify the most salient characteristics of their services and settings. Human service workers who view themselves as technicians offering consistent services to a wide range of clients might be able to use mechanistic organizational structures, but such designs would be inappropriate for professionals attempting to deliver multifaceted services based on community needs assessments. Helpers would also need to determine whether their environments were characterized more by rapid change or by stability over time, recognizing that agencies dealing with shifting populations or subject to changes in funding could not afford to use slow-moving, unwieldy organizational structures.

SUMMARY

A rich history of theory of organizations has guided organizational behavior in a wide range of settings. The classical models of bureaucracy, scientific management, and human relations as well as more current approaches such as the human resources models of Likert, McGregor, and Argyris and systems theory all have relevance today. New developments such as Japanese management, the excellence movement, and reinventing government initiatives have all affected the human services. Human service managers do use theory, consciously or unconsciously, and they are likely to be more effective if they consciously apply appropriate theories: the contingency theory approach. Being aware of a variety of theoretical frameworks helps human service professionals know that, as they seek to organize their programs, they do have choices. The theories discussed here should offer guidance to those who are designing or redesigning an agency so that all the various components will work effectively and efficiently together. We will now look at how organizations may be designed, based on thoughtful use of organizational theories.

DISCUSSION QUESTIONS

Chapter 4 discussed several approaches to organizational design, including (1) classical, bureaucratic theories, (2) human resources approaches, (3) contingency theories, (4) open systems theory, (5) Japanese management, and (6) newer models including excellence and reengineering.

1. Do you find some of these theories more helpful than others?

2. What theories do you see being used, explicitly or implicitly, in an organization with which you are familiar? Are these the appropriate theories to be used? If not, which ones would be better?

3. If you were designing a human service organization, which theories would you be most likely to use?

Case 4 | THE COMMUNITY CAREER CENTER

The Community Career Center (CCC) had been initiated several years ago by a group of professionals who became impatient with the impersonality and red tape that overwhelmed their work in public agencies. All four of the center's founders had previously worked for departments of human resources or vocational rehabilitation, and their experiences had led them to think that there must be better ways to deal with clients' career development needs.

A few basic concepts had been part of the center's orientation since it had first begun operation under Department of Labor and fee-based funding. First, the founders felt that one counselor should work with the total scope of a client's career needs, linking him or her with training programs, with educational institutions, with other needed services, and, finally, with jobs. They also believed in using training formats to deal with the kinds of needs many clients shared. From its unassuming start, the center had provided training programs dealing with midlife career change, retirement planning, job-hunting skills, self-assessment, and a variety of other topics. These programs were offered to members of the general public, such as women reentering the job market, and to local institutions and businesses.

At first, the founders of the center provided most of the services themselves. If they felt that a particular training format had exciting possibilities or if they were invited to design something special for a local group, they would provide workshops and group sessions. In the meantime, each of the four also carried a caseload of clients to whom they were dedicated. They saw themselves as counselors, advocates, and placement specialists for their own clients, and their success exceeded even their own idealistic expectations.

Last year, the center's management had begun to get out of hand. Its size had mushroomed, and so had its funding. Local businesses had proven so supportive, especially in contracting training programs, that the initial Department of Labor contract provided only a small percentage of the agency's total funding. Each training program was self-supporting, and the number of individual clients kept growing. To keep pace, the center had had to hire additional staff members to provide services, so there were now a number of trainers and counselors who had not been in on the original planning. Little by little, the original four founders had

become frustrated. Instead of spending all their time with clients and trainees, they were becoming involved in keeping books, planning repetitive services, and supervising staff members. This supervision especially bothered them. New staff members somehow did not understand the concept of being dedicated to their clients. These counselors did their work, but they were not bubbling over with creativity. They were not seeking new challenges, coming up with new ideas, or making that extra effort that made the difference. The original founders, who did have that urge for creativity, were unable to use it. They had become managers, and they did not like it.

The solution they had found last year was to bring in a business manager, a recent MBA, who knew how to organize and control a growing firm. The center's founders breathed a collective sigh of relief when management concerns were taken out of their hands. They gave their new manager a free hand and were pleased with the way he took control of the budgets and financial reports. The new organizational structure that he created also seemed to make sense. He divided the center into departments, including the training department, where programs were designed and implemented; the marketing department, which had responsibility for selling the training programs to industrial and other organizations; the counseling department, which provided direct services to clients; the job development department, which canvassed the community for placement possibilities for clients; and the business department, which took care of administrative concerns, including personnel.

This approach seemed to work for a while. The newer staff members, in particular, seemed pleased with the increased clarity of their job descriptions. They were no longer badgered with instructions to "be creative." They knew what their responsibilities were and could carry them out. The center's founders—still the board of directors of the agency—were pleased to have management responsibilities taken out of their hands. Now they could be creative again.

Yet that sense of renewed creativity had not taken hold. Somehow the agency's new organization did not allow for it. Now in its fifth year of existence, the Community Career Center was in jeopardy, not because it had failed but because it had succeeded. Two of the four board members wanted to resign and spin off a new smaller, more responsive agency. Monica Shannon and Paul Ramirez did not really want to make this move, but they could see no way to carry out what they believed to be their mission through an organization as unwieldy as the CCC had become.

At the most volatile meeting ever held at the center, the board of directors cleared the air. Shannon, one of the two original members who had decided to leave, spoke first.

"Look," she exclaimed, "our original idea was to have an agency that would be responsive to our clients' career needs. We would stick with an individual, be an ombudsman, help meet all this one client's needs. Now we have a department for counseling and another department for finding jobs. What happened to the idea that got us started in the first place?"

"And what about the training component?" Ramirez chimed in. "The idea was to meet community needs by designing special sessions, not to keep repeating the same program all the time to make it easier for the marketing department. Everything we do lately is to please the marketers, to make it easier for them to sell. But what have they got to sell? We've got the tail wagging the dog."

"Now, wait a minute," Mark Morgenstein responded. "We've got a big organization here. We can't expect everything to be the same as it was. Growth and change was supposed to be one of our big aims, too."

"And you were the ones who got the most excited about bringing in a manager to take the business responsibilities out of your hands," Colleen Morgan pointed out. "You can't have everything."

"I'll tell you one thing," Shannon said. "We may be a large organization now, but we accomplished more in a day when the four of us began than that whole gang of bureaucrats we've got here now accomplishes in a month. That's what we've got here now: a bureaucracy. Why did we ever bother leaving the Department of Human Resources? We've got a duplication right here."

1. Would you describe the Community Career Center's current organization as a bureaucracy? How does it compare with the structure that the agency had at first?
2. The agency grew in size over the years. What organizational theories should guide the organization at this stage?
3. At this point, do you think Monica Shannon and Paul Ramirez are right in wanting to leave the organization? What options do they have?

REFERENCES

12manage.com. (2005). *Organizational configurations: Mintzberg.* Retrieved September 2005 from 12manage.com at http://www.12manage.com/methods_mintzberg_configurations.html.2322222.

Accel-Team (2005a). *Elton Mayo: Findings.* Retrieved September 2005 from http://www.accel-team.com/human_relations/hrels_01_mayo.html.

Accel-Team (2005b). *Open systems approach to OD.* Retrieved September 2005 from http://www.accel-team.com/ltzpubz_10mxAT1005/atPDF_06_openSystems.pdf.

Ammons, D. (1998). Benchmarking performance. In S. Condrey (Ed.), *Handbook of human resource management in government* (pp. 391–409). San Francisco: Jossey-Bass.

Argyris, C. (1957). *Personality and organization.* New York: Harper & Row.

Bombyk, M. (1995). Progressive social work. In R. Edwards (Ed.), *Encyclopedia of social work* (19th ed., pp. 1933–1942). Washington, DC: NASW Press.

Bowditch, J., & Buono, A. (2005). *A primer on organizational behavior* (6th ed.). Hoboken, NJ: Wiley.

Bryson, J. (1995). *Strategic planning for public and nonprofit organizations.* San Francisco: Jossey-Bass.

Burns, T., & Stalker, G. (1994). *The management of innovation* (rev. ed.). New York: Oxford University Press.

Chandler, A. (1962). *Strategy and structure: Chapters in the history of the industrial enterprise.* Cambridge, MA: MIT Press.

Child, J. (1995). Follett: Constructive conflict. In P. Graham (Ed.), *Mary Parker Follett: Prophet of management* (pp. 87–95). Boston: Harvard Business School Press.

Cohen, B., & Austin, M. (1994). Organizational learning and change in a public child welfare agency. *Administration in Social Work, 18*(1), 1–18.

Cooke, R. A., & Rousseau, D. M. (1988). Behavioral norms and expectations: A quantitative approach to the assessment of organizational culture. *Group and Organization Studies, 13*(3), 245–273.

Fayol, H. (1949). *General and industrial management.* London: Sir Isaac Pitman.

Gerth, H. H., & Mills, C. W. (Eds.). (1958). *From Max Weber: Essays in sociology.* New York: Oxford University Press.

Gilson, S. (1997). The YWCA women's advocacy program: A case study of domestic violence and sexual assault services. *Journal of Community Practice, 4*(4), 1–26.

Gortner, H., Mahler, J., & Nicholson, J. (1997). *Organization theory: A public perspective* (2nd ed.). Fort Worth, TX: Harcourt Brace College Publishers.

Graham, P. (Ed.). (1995). *Mary Parker Follett: Prophet of management.* Boston: Harvard Business School Press.

Gummer, B., & McCallion, P. (Eds.). (1995). *Total quality management.* Albany, NY: Professional Development Program of Rockefeller College.

Hammer, M., & Champy, J. (1993). *Reengineering the corporation.* New York: HarperBusiness.

Harvey, C. (1998). Defining excellence in human service organizations. *Administration in Social Work, 22*(1), 33–45.

Hawkins, F., & Gunther, J. (1998). Managing for quality. In R. Edwards, J. Yankey, & M. Altpeter (Eds.), *Skills for effective management of nonprofit organizations* (pp. 525–554). Washington, DC: NASW Press.

Holleb, G., & Abrams, W. (1975). *Alternatives in community mental health.* Boston: Beacon.

Keys, P. (1995a). Japanese quality management techniques. In L. Ginsberg & P. Keys (Eds.), *New management in human services* (2nd ed., pp. 162–170). Washington, DC: NASW Press.

Keys, P. (1995b). Quality management. In R. Edwards (Ed.), *The encyclopedia of social work* (19th ed., pp. 2019–2025). Washington, DC: NASW Press.

Kurtz, P. (1998). A case study of a network as a learning organization. *Administration in Social Work, 22*(2), 57–73.

Lawrence, P. R., & Lorsch, J. (1967). *Organization and environment.* Cambridge, MA: Harvard University Press.

Likert, R. (1967). *The human organization: Its management and value.* New York: McGraw-Hill.

Mangier, M. (1999, July 24). Japanese firms use bullying to thin their ranks. *Los Angeles Times,* Section 1, pp. 1, 11.

McGregor, D. (1960). *The human side of enterprise.* New York: McGraw-Hill.

Micklethwait, J., & Wooldridge, A. (1997). *The witch doctors: Making sense of the management gurus.* New York: Times Books.

Miles, R. (1965). Human relations or human resources? *Harvard Business Review, 9*(43), 148–152.

Miles, R. (1975). *Theories of management: Implications for organizational behavior and development.* New York: McGraw Hill.

Mintzberg, H. (1979). *The structuring of organizations.* Upper Saddle River, NJ: Prentice Hall.

Mintzberg, H. (1992). *Structure in fives: Designing effective organizations.* Englewood Cliffs, NJ: Prentice Hall.

National Assembly of National Voluntary Health and Social Welfare Organizations. (1989). *A study in excellence: Management in the nonprofit human services.* Washington, DC: Author

Osborne, D., & Gaebler, T. (1992). *Reinventing government: How the entrepreneurial spirit is transforming the public sector.* Reading, MA: Addison-Wesley.

Osborne, D., & Plastrik, P. (1997). *Banishing bureaucracy: The five strategies for reinventing government.* Reading, MA: Addison-Wesley.

Ouchi, W. G. (1982). *Theory Z: How American business can meet the Japanese challenge.* New York: Avon.

Perlmutter, F. (Ed.). (1988). *Alternative social agencies: Administrative strategies.* New York: Haworth.

Perlmutter, F. (1995). Administering alternative social programs. In L. Ginsberg & P. Keys (Eds.), *New management in human services* (2nd ed., pp. 203–218). Washington, DC: NASW Press.

Perrow, C. (1986). *Complex organizations: A critical essay* (3rd ed.). New York: Random House.

Peters, T. J., & Waterman, R. H., Jr. (1982). *In search of excellence.* New York: Harper & Row.

Sashkin, M. (1981). An overview of ten organizational and management theorists. In J. Jones & W. Pfeiffer (Eds.), *The 1981 annual handbook for group facilitators* (pp. 206–221). San Diego, CA: University Associates.

Schein, E. (1992). *Organizational culture and leadership* (2nd ed.). San Francisco: Jossey-Bass.

Schmidt, W., & Finnegan, J. (1992). *The race without a finish line: America's quest for total quality.* San Francisco: Jossey-Bass.

Selber, K., & Austin, D. (1997). Mary Parker Follett: Epilogue to or return of a social work management pioneer? *Administration in Social Work, 21*(1), 1–15.

Senge, P. (1990). *The fifth discipline: The art and practice of the learning organization.* New York: Doubleday Currency.

Senge, P., Kleiner, A., Roberts, C., Ross, R., Roth, G., & Smith, B. (1999). *The dance of change.* New York: Doubleday.

Senge, P., Roberts, C., Ross, R., Smith, B., & Kleiner, A. (1994). *The fifth discipline fieldbook.* New York: Currency Doubleday.

Syers, M. (1995). Follett, Mary Parker (1868–1933). In R. Edwards (Ed.), *The encyclopedia of social work* (19th ed., p. 2585). Washington, DC: NASW Press.

Taylor, F. W. (1911). *Principles of scientific management.* New York: Harper & Row.

Taylor, J., & Felten, D. (1993). *Performance by design.* Upper Saddle River, NJ: Prentice Hall.

Trice, H. M., & Beyer, J. M. (1993). *The cultures of work organizations.* Upper Saddle River, NJ: Prentice Hall.

Walton, R. (1975). Criteria for quality of working life. In L. Davis & A. Cherns (Eds.), *The quality of working life: Volume 1: Problems, prospects, and the state of the art* (pp. 91–118). New York: Free Press.

Weisbord, M. (1987). *Productive workplaces.* San Francisco: Jossey-Bass.

Zell, D. (1997). *Changing by design: Organizational innovation at Hewlett-Packard.* Ithaca, NY: ILR Press.

MODELS OF SERVICE DELIVERY | CHAPTER 4

© Louise Gubb/Corbis

47

After reading this chapter, you will be able to:

- Define three models of service delivery.
- Trace their development.
- Illustrate the use of these models in human service delivery today.
- Apply the three models to a human service problem.

Self-assessment

- Outline the differences among the medical model, the public health model, and the human service model.
- What principles of the medical model and/or the public health model are present in the human service model?
- Compare the treatment of mental illness in the three service delivery models.
- List the key factors that contributed to the development of the human service model.
- Describe how the three models might coordinate services to address a human service problem such as teen pregnancy.

In developing a definition of human services, we have discussed its various characterizations, briefly traced the history of service provision, and explored recent developments, emphasizing human services today. Another approach to defining human services is to examine the way it benefits service recipients. This chapter describes three models that represent different orientations in service delivery: the medical model, the public health model, and the human service model. The chapter concludes with a case that illustrates the interaction of these models.

In this chapter, you will meet clients who have received services delivered in the context of these three models. The cases of Robert Smith and Ralph Jones illustrate services provided by the medical model. Sean O'Reilly was a recipient of services provided by the public health model. Susan, her husband, Ted, and children, Matthew and Justin, illustrate the complexities of client needs, needs that may require multi-faceted, long-term intervention.

All three models are used to deliver services today, and depending on the problem, an integration of all three models may be most effective. In practice, some agencies may prefer one over the others, and one model may be more effective than the other two in some situations. Workers may be skilled in following one particular model, but they are likely to be working closely with practitioners who follow the other models. Therefore, you should know the characteristics of each model, its historical development, and how it is used. To help translate this information into human service practice, we examine a relevant social problem from the perspective of each model.

Each of the three models of service delivery has certain philosophical assumptions that guide its practice. These assumptions reflect beliefs about the causes of problems, their treatment, and the role of the professional in the model. To illustrate, we consider the nature of mental disorders from the perspectives of each of the three models.

The medical model is based on an orientation developed by the medical profession; it assumes that mental disorders are diseases or illnesses that impair an individual's ability to function. The disease or illness, in this case the mental disorder, has an organic basis and responds to medical interventions such as medication, laboratory studies, and physical therapies. Often the individual, or **patient**, receives treatment from a physician in a hospital or medical clinic.

The public health model resembles the medical model in its diagnosis and treatment process, but the models differ in recipients of services and methodologies of treatment. Whereas the medical model emphasizes individuals, the public health model focuses on *groups* in the population who may be identified by geography (community, country, region, or state), types of problems (abuse, poverty, specific illnesses), or specific characteristics such as age (children, the elderly). This model views mental disorders as the result of malfunctions or pressures created by the environment or by society. The mental disorder is evaluated for its impact not only on the individual but also on society at large. In addition to treating the individual, this model emphasizes preventing the problem through supporting activities such as use of films, speakers, school programs, and pamphlets, all aimed at educating the population about the problem.

The **human service model** is concerned with the interaction between the individual and the environment, stressing the need for balance between the two. Although recognizing both the medical and the public health perspectives, this model focuses on the interpersonal and environmental conflicts that may result from the problem (in this case, a mental disorder). Perhaps the individual (or **client** or **consumer**) has problems resulting from genetic predispositions, biochemical imbalances, faulty learning, lack of insight into behavior that may be inappropriate, a physical or mental disability, and/or influences from the social environment. Whatever the situation, the client is experiencing interpersonal and emotional difficulties that affect behavior. Treatment in this model encompasses services to both the individual and the environment through work with the client as well as the people and the institutions with which the client is involved. An important consideration in the model is the focus on client strengths rather than inadequacies. Each model provides a different perspective on the same problem. We now look at the development of each one.

THE MEDICAL MODEL

Definition

The **medical model** sees the person coming for help as an individual whose problem is a disease or a sickness. The individual is "sick" or "ill," not healthy. Often called *patients,* these individuals depend on the physician or service provider to prescribe a treatment or cure for the "disease." Historically, this model can be summarized as a system that involves the following elements: symptom–diagnosis–treatment–cure (Reinhard, 1986).

The medical model, with a history that includes shamans, medicine men and women, and witch doctors, is perhaps the oldest of all treatment models. In fact, other models used it as they were developing. For example, in Chapter 2 we discussed the beginning of the new profession of social work at the turn of the 20th century. Mary Richmond, author of *Social Diagnosis* (1917), used the medical model to describe social casework. Believing that the presenting problem was rooted in the individual, she suggested that pauperism was a disease. The friendly visitor,

49

BOX 4.1

INTERNATIONAL FOCUS
Models of Service Design

Thinking about models of service design in developing countries, Howard N. Higginbotham (1979) suggested three basic models of service design today: traditional psychiatry, the public health approach, and the village system. He believed that the "the first model, traditional **psychiatry**, is similar to North American or European psychiatry, which has not been modified for use in non-Western settings." The focus of this model includes using residential facilities that means that recipients must travel to find help. Residential services range from long-term confinement or therapy like farming or doing daily chores. New admits and long-term clients may receive psychotropic medication and electroconvulsive shock therapy (ECT); few patients receive traditional **psychotherapy**.

The second model is a public health approach to services where prevention and training volunteers or paraprofessionals is emphasized. Patients are helped outside a residential settings using consultation with family and education of the patient and the family and other community resources.

Because the Western models have not worked well in developing countries, the village system has emerged as a viable option to treatment for those with mental illness. It uses native healers, therapeutic relationships, psychotropic drugs, and the natural therapeutic elements of the village, which include confession, dancing, and rituals.

Source: Adapted from "Culture and Mental Services," by Howard N. Higginbotham. In Anthony J. Marsella, Roland G. Tharp, and Thomas Ciborowski (Eds.), *Perspectives on Cross-Cultural Psychology*, pp. 205–236. Copyright © 1979 by Academic Press.

therefore, became a social physician whose duty was to heal the complex conditions of poverty (Zimbalist, 1977).

The corrections field also adopted the medical model during the 1930s, when its emphasis shifted from punishment to treatment. The change was based on the assumption that criminal behavior was the result of physical or environmental aspects of an individual's life, requiring treatment (Clear, Cole, & Resig, 2005). Theoretically, prisons were to become therapeutic communities, where inmates would be rehabilitated to reenter society. Unfortunately, budget constraints limited this change to one of name only: Departments of prisons became "departments of corrections," but punishment continued to be the reality. Structurally, the system already included parole, probation, and the indeterminate sentence. All that remained to complete the incorporation of the medical model was the addition of a classification system to aid in diagnosis and treatment (Clear et al., 2005).

HISTORY

As mentioned in Chapter 2, institutions developed as a way to meet the needs of some segments of society. Asylums were established primarily to care for people with mental illness, shifting care from the local community to rural institutions and replacing local financing with state funding. Responsibility for the care of people with mental illness rested with the medical profession.

Psychiatry emerged as a discipline at the end of the 18th century when Philippe Pinel became head of the Hospice de Bicêtre and later of Salpetriere (mental institutions in France). Some mental disorders had been recognized as such early on, but Pinel's removal of chains from patients and other humane acts emphasized the belief

50

that pathological behavioral disorders had organic origins and that their treatment belonged to medicine. Accordingly, those diagnosed as mentally ill were to be treated as patients by physicians in hospital settings, just like other patients with medical problems. Pinel, hoping to create a science of mental disease, is credited with introducing the medical model into psychiatry by stressing the clinical diagnosis and appropriate medical treatment. (See Box 4.2.)

Until the end of the 19th century, insanity was socially defined: "An insane was a person whose behavior for pathological reasons was so disturbed that he had to be segregated in special institutions" (Pichot, 1985, p. 10). With the emergence of psychiatry as a medical specialty, a body of knowledge was established to explain the nature and causes of insanity. The discovery and application of the most effective treatments became a priority. Insanity became medically defined, meaning that the institution of treatment had to be a hospital instead of a prison, and the care of the patient would be handled by a physician, not a warden.

After the middle of the 19th century, use of the medical model to treat mental illness dominated. By the end of the century, however, the medical model was changing. A new school of thought rejected medical treatment and advocated psychotherapy for treatment of people with mental illness. The new philosophy was based on the assumption that diseases of the soul were completely separate from diseases of the body. Psychiatry concerned itself with the medicine of the soul; psychosis was the disease of the soul, and **neurosis** was the disease of the nerves (Pichot, 1985). Sigmund Freud's work reflected this orientation.

Early in his career, Freud was a researcher and clinician in biology and neurology; he made outstanding contributions to both fields. He used the scientific method, insisting that medical problems of mental illness be studied in the rigorous laboratory setting. Later, Freud rejected his earlier training and revolutionized the study and treatment of mental illness. He developed a method of therapy commonly known today as the **psychoanalytic method**. In this method, the clients/patients share all thoughts with the therapist. The therapist interprets this material to explain to patients the nature of their repressions and the influence of these repressions on their present problems. Freud also developed a theory of neurosis and one of the normal mind, based on the assumption that mental disorders were psychologically rooted.

Although Freud's impact was profound, psychoanalytic theory did not completely change the medical model or become the preferred method of treatment, for several reasons. First, its success was difficult to evaluate and to document. Second, it required too much time and expense to be a viable treatment for large numbers of people.

The treatment of people with mental illness continued to develop in the 1940s; however, more psychiatrists and improved treatment were needed. A common treatment during this decade was electroconvulsive or **electroshock therapy**. This treatment involved administering an electric shock of 70 to 130 volts to the brain, leaving the patient unconsciousness and/or in convulsions. On regaining consciousness, the patient sometimes experienced confusion and memory loss, but problem behaviors diminished after several weeks of treatments. Electroshock therapy was effective with depressed individuals, but it was used less successfully to treat other mental disorders. Its abuse during the 1960s resulted in negative perceptions of this treatment method, and these perceptions contributed to the growing popularity of psychotropic medications.

51

BOX 4.2 | PHILIPPE PINEL

Philippe Pinel (1745–1826) is famous in the history of medicine and mental health. In revolutionary France, Pinel courageously campaigned to secure a new status for persons with mental illness as people suffering from disease rather than being possessed by demons or manifesting the consequences of sin. Pinel argued, practiced, and taught that such persons require medical care rather than persecution or punishment, and that they are entitled to be treated with respect as persons and citizens. This was a revolutionary idea.

Pinel was born into a modest family of surgeons in southwestern France. Initially trained as a cleric and destined for service in the church, he decided to study science in Toulouse. By 1773, he had acquired a doctorate of medicine, but he continued his studies for four more years in Montpellier under Barthez. Sickness and health became his lifelong concern, and he systematically applied himself to learning all he could about medicine from ancient as well as contemporary sources. He acquired the education of a classicist and a humanist in addition to his extensive knowledge of the practice of medicine in his day. He moved to Paris in 1778 and supported himself by translating scientific and medical works and teaching mathematics.

Though extremely shy, he became a member of an important group of reformers and medical thinkers called the Ideologues. Benjamin Franklin tried to convince Pinel to go to America. However, Pinel was a patriot and wished to help modernize medicine in his own country. His interest in insanity derived from the suicide of a seriously depressed friend and patient in 1783. In 1792, apparently because of his connections with the Ideologues, Pinel was appointed Physician of the Infirmaries to the Hospice de Bicetre, a huge Parisian custodial institution for indigent ailing men.

During this time, Pinel published three significant works: *Philosophical Nosography* (1798), *Treatise on Insanity* (1801), and *Clinical Medicine* (1802). The first book would serve for years as a text for the classification of diseases; the second would lay the foundation for modern psychiatry; and the third, published in three successively enlarged editions, would spread his methodology and fame among the next generation.

In 1794, Pinel transferred to the Hospice de la Salpetriere, an institution that housed nearly 7,000 destitute women. He administered, practiced, and taught in this hospital for 30 years, applying the principles that gave him the reputation as a founder of modern psychiatry.

In medical practice, Pinel practically invented the role of the full-time resident physician who teaches and trains students, interns, and fellow researchers in a hospital ward. Along with other reformers, he argued for national curricula, standards, and diplomas for medical education. Pinel insisted that such education should be conducted in French and based on clinical practice and observations. He viewed the natural sciences as "accessories" to the practice of medicine.

With regard to mental health, Pinel is often given credit for what he learned from the uneducated but experienced and successful Keeper of the Insane at Bicetre, J. P. Pussin (1746–1811): namely, that the mental patients could be managed without cages, chains, or cruelty. Pinel brought Pussin to Salpetriere in 1802 to aid him in caring for the many unruly patients. Pinel combined Pussin's practical management principles with his own medical knowledge to develop his famous "moral method" for treating mental illness. This method assumes that mental illness is due to some imbalance in the patient, which the physician can treat and rectify. The crux of this method is extensive observation and knowledge about the patient. This knowledge makes possible detailed therapy, which the physician must carefully supervise. Pinel's approach is a far cry from bleeding, beating, purging, and imprisonment, which had been the usual methods of treating the insane.

Pinel's methods and publications made him well known, and students flocked to him. Among them were the future leaders of French medicine. Pinel's concern for humane treatment of persons with mental illness was realized in France and made that country a world leader in the enlightened treatment of mental illness. When Dorothea Dix traveled in Europe in the late 1850s, extending her great American crusade to reform in the treatment of the insane, she had only small changes to recommend to the French, and to the Turks in Constantinople who had been trained by the French.

Source: Used by permission of H. Phillips Hamlin (1985).

Psychotropic drugs, which act on the brain, are now among the most widely used treatments for mental disorders. Many human service professionals work with clients taking psychotropic medications and need to be knowledgeable about the drugs their clients are taking. The science of the preparation, uses, and effects of drugs is pharmacology. The branch of pharmacology of most interest to human service professionals is **psychopharmacology,** which focuses on "the psychological effects of drugs and the use of drugs to treat symptoms of mental and emotional disorders" (Ingersoll & Rak, 2006, p. 3).

One example of the necessity for knowledge about psychotropic drugs is on-label and off-label prescriptions. On-label means that the drug has been approved by the Food and Drug Administration (FDA) to treat a specific disorder; however, many psychotropic drugs are prescribed off-label. This means that they are not specifically approved by the FDA for a certain disorder. Rather, the medical professional believes, based on case studies and other evidence, that the drug will help the condition or disorder the client has. Neither label guarantees a drug is totally safe or effective for everyone.

Psychotropic medications can be divided into four major classes: antipsychotic drugs, antidepressant drugs, antianxiety drugs, and lithium salts. **Antipsychotic drugs** are effective in managing psychotic disorders such as bipolar disorder (colloquially known as manic depression) and schizophrenia. Although these drugs do not cure psychosis, they help to control certain psychotic behaviors such as suspiciousness, hallucinations, and impulsiveness. Haldol (haloperidol), Stelaxine (trifluoperazine), Thorazine (chlorpromazine), Clozaril (clozapine), and Mellaril (thioridazine) are well-known examples of antipsychotic medication.

Antidepressant drugs, the second class, relieve depression. There are two kinds of antidepressant drugs: the tricyclic antidepressants and the monoamine oxidase inhibitors. Human service workers will most likely come in contact with widely used tricyclic antidepressants such as Elavil (amitriptyline) or Tofranil (imipramine); however, Prozac (fluoxetine), Paxil (paroxetine), Luvor (fluvoxamine), and Zoloft (sertraline)—antidepressants unrelated to tricyclic or monoamine oxidase inhibitors—have become increasingly popular in recent years because of fewer side effects. These drugs are selective seratonin reuptake inhibitors (SSRIs).

The most widely used psychotropic medications by far are the **antianxiety drugs,** *sedatives,* and *hypnotics.* Prescribed to relieve anxiety, fear, or tension, these medications may be classed as barbiturates, benzodiazepines, or antihistamines. Benzodiazepines such as Valium (diazepam), Klonopin (clonazepam), Xanax (alprazolam), Tranxene (clorazepate), and Librium (chlordiazepoxide) are especially popular because they reduce anxiety without reducing overall performance.

The final class of psychotropic medication is **mood stabilizers.** They include lithium carbonate, calcium channel blockers (Calan, Isoptin), and anticonvulsants (Tegretol, Epitol). Used primarily in the treatment of bipolar disorder, these drugs are particularly effective in preventing the mania state, which is characterized by symptoms of extreme irritability, talkativeness, grandiose ideas, exaggerated self-esteem, and increased involvement in risky activities such as spending sprees or reckless driving.

Psychotropic medications have revolutionized mental health by facilitating deinstitutionalization, but the effects have not always been positive. For example, critics

53

TABLE 4.1	POSSIBLE SIDE EFFECTS OF PSYCHOTROPIC MEDICATIONS

Antipsychotic Drugs	Convulsions
Feelings of heaviness	**Antianxiety drugs**
Sluggishness	Drug tolerance
Weakness	Stumbling gait
Faintness	Slurred speech
Drowsiness	Drowsiness
Dizziness	Conjunctivitis
Tremors	Dry mouth
Seizures	Constipation
Tardive dyskinesia	Urinary problems
Loss of muscle tone	**Mood stabilizers**
Antidepressants	Toxic warning signs (nausea, tremors, muscle spasms)
Dry mouth	Thyroid disorders
Blurred vision	Renal toxicity
Constipation	Nausea
Urinary retention	Vomiting
Lowered or raised blood pressure	Diarrhea
Agitation	Sedation
Raised temperature	Confusion
Hallucinations	

say that antianxiety drugs mask symptoms so that individuals avoid dealing with the real problem. Clients who take major tranquilizers over a long period of time may suffer dangerous side effects, such as tardive dyskinesia, a neurological disorder characterized by abnormal, involuntary mouth or tongue movements. Table 4.1 lists other common side effects of the four major categories.

Today, those who deliver services in the medical model face several challenges. One is that the symptom–diagnosis–treatment–cure process more realistically leads to cure *or* control. Particularly with psychiatric illnesses, controlling the symptoms and making the patient functional are the guides for treatment. Complicating this issue are the numerous new drugs that appear with frequency. There are now many drugs that do not fit neatly into the four categories of psychotropic drugs just described. For example, the serotonin drugs (Prozac, Paxil, and Zoloft), which do not fit in one category, are broadly prescribed today to treat bulimia, obsessive-compulsive disorders, and anxiety disorders.

BOX 4.3	WEB SOURCES
	Find Out More about Psychotropic Medications

www.npi.ucla.edu/mhdd/INFO/modules/
psychotropicmedsoverview.html

This site outlines psychotropic medications, their uses, and frequently asked questions about them.

www.cqc.state.ny.us/

New York State has prepared a website that offers the latest information on best practices, client/customer services, what's new, and other topics about quality care for the mentally disabled. "Could This Happen in Your Program?" provides a number of cases to challenge and spark reflection and discussion among direct-care staff about policies and practices.

www.applesforhealth.com/psymedchild1.html

This site describes the current information on the safety and efficacy of medications for children and adolescents with mental disorders. Data by NIMH provide advanced knowledge of the effects of psychotropic drugs on children.

www.mental-health-today.com

This site provides current articles about mental health treatment and psychotropic medications.

www.mentalhealth.com

This site provides an extensive list of psychotropic medications, their descriptions, indications, contraindications, warnings, adverse effects, dosage, and research findings.

A second challenge is determining who controls medical services. Is it the physician, the patient, insurers or managed care organizations, employers, and/or the government? To varying degrees, all seem to have a role. For example, the intrusions of government become greater each year. Although it is sometimes difficult medically to separate the organic and psychiatric states, it has happened at some state government levels; that is, diagnosis and reimbursement guidelines have differentiated physical and mental conditions. A second example is the impact of managed care discussed in Chapter 3. Typically, in a managed system, physicians receive a fixed amount per patient to take care of medical problems. A small part of the capitation fee is for behavioral health care. Once again, physicians are faced with an arbitrary separation between physical and psychiatric conditions. They also grapple daily with wanting to do the right thing but at the same time contain costs. Achieving this balance is difficult when physicians attend to the "whole" patient, which includes a consideration of the patient's environment and social circumstances. In some instances, physicians have lost their right to choose which drugs to prescribe because managed care staff overrule their recommendations in favor of less expensive medicines.

The past 30 years have demystified psychiatric illness and made its acceptance widespread. The future may include new perspectives. One may be an awareness that we treat mild disease too aggressively. A second perspective is that in some cases it is society that is malfunctional, not the individual—that is, society places people in situations that are not normal but expects them not to behave abnormally. For example, think about the malfunctional mother who has a full-time job as well as responsibility for the home and the children. The problem may not be that she is malfunctional but that society's expectations are unrealistic.

| TABLE 4.2 | SUMMARY POINTS: HISTORY OF THE MEDICAL MODEL |

- Individual is "sick."
- Recipient is called *patient*.
- 18th-century Philippe Pinel removes chains of mentally ill.
- Pinel stresses clinical diagnosis and treatment.
- Psychiatry emerges as a medical specialty.
- Mid-19th-century psychotherapy emerges as treatment.
- Freud develops psychoanalytic method.
- Electric shock is introduced in the 1940s.
- Psychotropic drugs become the most widely used treatments.

CASE STUDIES

One obvious example of the medical model's application to human service problems is its use in treating mental illness. Two illustrative case studies follow. The case of Robert Smith describes the mental illness and treatment of a man in the late 1870s. This narrative not only illustrates the orientation of the medical model but also expresses the attitudes of that time toward mental illness. The case of Ralph Jones represents the use of the medical model over 100 years later. The use of the medical model in the second case is especially reflected in the prescription of medication and other physical treatments for Ralph's illness. In both cases, note that the clients are considered ill and that their treatment reflects this diagnosis.

ROBERT SMITH

Robert Smith was the fourth of six children and the third son. His family, third-generation immigrants from England, lived in Philadelphia. Robert was quiet and withdrawn as a child, and while he did the work the family found for him, he was never very energetic in seeking it out.

The Smith family was relatively poor. Their fortunes improved somewhat during the Civil War, when they were able to find employment in the war-related metal industry, but after the war they descended again into poverty.

In his late 20s, Robert began to have episodes of "mania," as a doctor later called it. While still usually quiet and withdrawn, Robert would become violent and aggressive if crossed by members of his family or neighbors or if frustrated by events. These episodes of mania cost him his job, and soon the family was having to watch him all the time. During an episode, he would sometimes attack anyone who tried to communicate with him; when the episode passed, he would again become withdrawn and listless.

When Robert's aggressiveness began to be expressed toward the neighbors as well as toward family members, the family began to seek help for him. They took him to physicians, who examined him but did not know what to do for him. By the time he was 32, Robert Smith's behavior had become so distressing that his family was desperate. He had been arrested more than once for destroying property in the neighborhood and threatening neighbors. His family had only barely kept him out of prison. His father took him to the county commission, which, after hearing the testimony of the family and the local

56

sheriff, agreed to send him to the Blockley Almshouse in the fall of 1875. Blockley Alms-house was a huge collection of buildings maintained by the city of Philadelphia for its insane poor. When it was time for Robert to go there, the combined efforts of several family members and neighbors were necessary to overcome his resistance and subdue him.

At first, Robert was kept in the general hospital to recover from the injuries he had received in resisting the move to Blockley. Then he was transferred to a crowded asylum building, where he was nominally under the care of Dr. Isaac Ray, whom he actually never saw except from a distance. Robert had to sleep on a night bed put on the floor in a corridor. When his violent episodes occurred, he was put in a straight waistcoat, which reduced his ability to attack other patients or attendants. The ward was generally noisy and turbulent. There was little chance for a good night's sleep, nor was there anything much for the patients to do during the day except to excite each other, creating almost continual disturbances.

After a year in Blockley, and weeks in a straitjacket, Robert became less violent and more depressed. Cold-water treatments seemed to reduce his violent episodes while he was in Blockley. His family noticed that he had lost weight and they became worried about his physical health. They found the hospital dreary and depressing, but they were reluctant to have Robert discharged because they were afraid of what he would do outside. They were torn by their desire to get help for him and their concern that conditions at Blockley were unhealthy.

In the fall of 1876, the Smiths decided to move to Albany, New York. Because Robert seemed more manageable, if not better, they decided to take him with them. He made the journey all right, but the new environment seemed to bring on upsetting manic episodes such as he had had in Philadelphia. Within months, the family was again trying to decide what to do with him.

The business they had joined, begun by Mr. Smith's oldest brother, was modestly successful, so the family's financial resources were improved. When Robert's condition worsened, his family took him to a well-known local physician. After futile attempts to treat Robert, the doctor suggested that they take him to the Lunatic Asylum for the State of New York at Utica. The physician assured them that this asylum was a reputable one, much better than Blockley, and he signed a Certificate of Insanity, which helped them get Robert's admission to the asylum approved by a justice of the court.

In the early summer of 1877, Robert was taken to Utica by his father, uncle, and two older brothers. They traveled by boat, a short distance up the Hudson River, and then west on the Mohawk, a journey of some 150 miles.

The Smiths were impressed and encouraged by the asylum at Utica. They were shown the ward where Robert would stay; it was large, cheerful, and well furnished with large windows. None of the other patients were in straitjackets, and the Smiths were told that Dr. Gray, the superintendent, did not believe in mechanical restraints. Rather, he believed in an organized regimen of treatment that involved engaging the patients' minds and bodies in healthy activities, such as walking, bowling, gardening, and the mechanical arts.

Robert improved somewhat at Utica. The frequency and intensity of his manic episodes decreased, and within a year he was able to go home on a parole of about six months. However, he was never able to remain outside the asylum longer than that because his mania would return and intensify. He spent most of his remaining life in the asylum at Utica and died in 1890 from pneumonia, which he caught after a bout with influenza (Hamlin, 1985).

RALPH JONES

Ralph Jones has had a hard life. The third youngest of seven children, he apparently witnessed the suicide of his natural mother when he was 6. His natural father was either

57

unable or unwilling to keep the family together, and all the children were sent to foster homes and orphanages.

Ralph was adopted at age 10 by a minister and a psychiatric social worker. He had a hard time getting along with them. He began dealing and using drugs when he was about 13 years old, abusing pot, phencyclidine (PCP), acid, and alcohol. He may have become an alcoholic by the age of 16. Ralph says that his adoptive parents were kind to him, but he just could not seem to do what they wanted, and after a while relations between them became very strained. At 16, Ralph was brought to the local youth program at the mental hospital because of his drug problems and violent acting out.

He did not complete high school but managed to get a GED while studying mechanics at a local vocational school and living in a group home. Ralph served 18 months in the Army. He was discharged with partial disability, caused by an injury to his left leg which he incurred playing football.

Ralph tends to be violent and lacks self-control when he has been drinking. Because of this behavior, he has lost many different jobs. Once, while drunk, he robbed and assaulted an elderly man in Florida—a crime for which he spent one year in jail. Also, he has been in several accidents, suffering injuries to his head and his back. He complains frequently of back pains.

Within the last five months, Ralph has been in jail twice and also in the state mental hospital. He was jailed on charges of driving while intoxicated. While there, he committed acts that were taken to be suicidal gestures. The first time, he cut his wrists superficially, and the second time, he slashed his throat with a razor blade. Both times, Ralph was brought straight from the jail to the mental hospital. The second incident occurred only three days before his jail term was to be completed.

A case review was undertaken after three weeks at the mental hospital. Admission notes were reviewed: Ralph was unclean, nonverbal, depressed, and lacking in judgment. He claimed to be suffering from alcohol withdrawal at the time of admission. The doctor who admitted him said that Ralph looked "psychotic" at the time.

A number of features of Ralph's situation came out during the case review. During his previous stay at the mental hospital, he had received shock treatments and was heavily sedated most of the time. He was given Thorazine, a tranquilizer used to control psychotic behaviors and calm patients down, and another drug to counter the side effects of Thorazine. The two psychiatrists he saw noted that he was uncooperative and lacked understanding of his suicidal, violent, alcoholic, abusive behavior.

Today his situation remains complex. First, Ralph admits to several suicide attempts or gestures, dating back to when he was 18, but he is not willing to talk about them other than to say that he is depressed all the time.

Second, he has a fiancée, whom he plans to marry within a year. She visits him regularly, dominates communication between him and the staff when she is around, and believes that he would be better off discharged. Also, she reports that he is well behaved, even gregarious, around her family. Ralph has virtually no other social contacts. She has been encouraging him to go to AA meetings and accompanies him when he does attend. In a conversation with a social worker, Ralph said he was afraid that she would press charges for a beating he gave her eight months ago.

Third, Ralph's contacts with his siblings and adoptive family have been minimal. He says he would like to live with his adoptive family, but they absolutely refuse to have anything to do with him. He has had no contact with any of his siblings in over two years.

Fourth, Ralph apparently does well at skilled manual work and is only about one term short of completing training as a mechanic at a vocational school. When asked about his plans for the future, he says that he wishes to complete his schooling, get a job, and then get married.

Fifth, he was married in his late teens and fathered two children (ages 7 and 8 now) before getting divorced at age 22. However, it is unknown where this family is and what connection, if any, he has with them.

Finally, it seems clear that Ralph is a depressed, angry person who can be dangerous to himself and others. His antisocial tendencies seem to have been established early in his life, and they are exacerbated by his alcohol problem. It is not at all clear that he has even begun to work through what was perhaps the central trauma of his childhood, his mother's suicide.

Two weeks ago Ralph was discharged and placed in a community halfway house. Ten days later he was readmitted to the mental hospital (three days ago) after he beat his roommate and then slashed his wrists. The treatment team, composed of a case manager, a nurse, a physician, a social worker, a psychologist, and a teacher, is not sure whether Ralph should be discharged again so that he can pursue the goals he articulates. The team is not convinced that he can handle life outside the hospital. The alcohol problem remains and seems to precipitate actions dangerous to Ralph and others; yet he still has goals, and apparently his fiancée remains supportive. If he were to establish a relationship with someone at a mental health center to secure help for him at his lowest points and if he were to attend AA meetings and stop abusing alcohol, some members of the treatment team believe that he might be able to get his life together and be placed in the community again (Hamlin, 1985).

These case studies describe two treatments of mental illness. As you answer the following questions, you will come to understand better the characteristics of the medical model.

- What problems did Robert Smith face? Ralph Jones?
- What treatments did Robert receive? Ralph?
- Why are these treatments classified as part of the medical model?

THE PUBLIC HEALTH MODEL

Definition

Public health is a concept that is sometimes difficult to define. One challenge in defining it is its multidisciplinary nature, which leads to difficulty in understanding it as a whole and defining its operations. We can approach the definition of public health in three ways. One is to define it by examining its historical development, achievements, and health successes. The next section will provide a brief review of this perspective. A second approach is to examine its goal, which is to provide the opportunities and conditions for health as a basic human right. This goal is reflected in its mission: to fulfill society's interest in assuring conditions in which people can be healthy (Committee Study of the Future of Public Health, 1988). Because the concept of health has changed during the 1800s and 1900s, a third approach to defining public health reflects its dynamism and adaptability. For example, until the past few decades, health has meant the absence of disease and disability. Today, health has a more positive meaning—the capacity to live fully, which entails maintaining the physical, mental, and social reserves for coping with life's circumstances in a way that brings satisfaction (Seligman, 2004).

The terrorist attacks on September 11, 2001, presented new challenges for public health. Many people feared a bioterrorist attack was next, and the government's basic lab facilities, computers, personnel, and training were found to be lacking. This state

59

of affairs prompted the rebuilding of the nation's public health system. "Dirty bombs," plague, anthrax, and smallpox have become part of our consciousness as serious threats to the population (Spake, 2003).

The **public health model** bridges the medical and human service models but is more obviously linked with the medical model. Diagnosis and treatment of individuals through the use of medicine and surgery are the core of clinical medicine. Physicians have delineated parts of the body (anatomy), how they function (physiology), their disorders (pathology), and the agents of disease (etiology). Their goal is to combat disease by repairing the breakdown of the "machinery" (Seligman, 2004). Those physicians who are cognizant of social, environmental, and biological factors and see disease as it affects populations have moved toward the public health model.

Public health is sometimes not separable from human welfare. Improving public health means improving education, nutrition, safe food and water supplies, immunization, and maternal and child health. It is particularly difficult to dissociate ill health from poverty.

In conclusion, a number of characteristics of the public health model distinguish it from the other two service delivery models. The public health model, like the medical model, is concerned with individuals who have problems, but it extends the concept of heath care beyond the traditional medical model. In the belief that individuals' problems may be linked to other social problems, the public health model serves larger populations rather than just individuals. Societal control is a prime concern of the public health model, as it attempts to solve many of society's social problems. In summary this model approaches social conditions by collecting data from the public and from examining individuals with problems.

The public health model applies a multicausal approach to studying the causes or origins of problems and emphasizes **prevention.** The preventive component also distinguishes this model from the medical model. The general aims of the American public health service system include not only a more equal distribution of health care services to all segments of the population (including the elderly, people with disabilities, and the impoverished) but also identification of social, nondisease problems and methods of attacking their causes and contributing factors. This is also the case in southern Africa, where HIV continues to spread. Public health efforts focused on prevention combine education about abstinence, condoms, and fidelity. The objective of the public health model is to improve the present and future quality of life and to alleviate health problems that have consequences for society in general.

HISTORY

Communicable diseases, poor sanitation, and lack of medical knowledge have been community health problems since ancient times. During the colonial period in North America, smallpox, yellow fever, and cholera were major health problems. Laws such as the Massachusetts Poor Law of 1692 gave local authorities the power to remove and isolate the afflicted. By the end of the 18th century, establishment of the first dispensaries and the first local boards of health had laid the foundations for voluntary organizations and public health agencies.

In the early 1800s, people migrated from the country to urban areas around burgeoning industrial plants. Severe disease outbreaks resulted from the poor nutrition, overcrowding, filth, and excessive work requirements of the inhabitants living in these slums. Lemuel Shattuck, a Boston city councilman, prepared a report financed by the Massachusetts legislature that presented the first plan for an integrated health program in the United States. The 1850 Shattuck Report in the United States precipitated both a sanitary awakening and social reform that constituted public health at that time (Afifi & Breslow, 1994).

The report declared the need for improved sanitation and disease control in Massachusetts and recommended establishment of state and local boards of health, collection of vital statistics, institution of sanitation programs, and prevention of disease (Shirreffs, 1982). Although widely ignored at the time, Shattuck's report has come to be considered the most farsighted and influential document in the history of the public health system (Committee Study of the Future of Public Health, 1988). By 1868, Massachusetts had established the first state public health department in the country.

The social philosophies of the early 19th century also impacted public health as they reflected two beliefs about disease. The first was that disease was providential. Like poverty and natural disasters such as floods, disease occurred as a result of God's wrath toward an individual. Therefore, the obvious solution to the problem was improved behavior. The second belief linked disease to the disorderly and filthy cities with their unpaved streets, poor drainage, untethered animals, and outside privies. Intuitively, people realized the impact of environmental factors on disease. Many believed that the solution was to eliminate dirt and filth to create a healthier environment.

A second important event was the organization in 1861 of the U.S. Sanitary Commission, the first major public health group in America. It is significant to the public health movement because its efforts were primarily preventive; it alerted the public to the benefits of preventive sanitary measures. Appalled by the poor conditions in army camps and hospitals, a group led by Dr. Henry Bellows, Louisa Schuyler, and Dr. Elisha Harris organized this voluntary citizen effort. A central focus of the commission was to unite all voluntary groups to aid governmental agencies in meeting the physical and spiritual needs of men in uniform. Initially, their efforts were directed toward teaching proper personal hygiene and inspecting and supervising living arrangements in camps and field hospitals. Their later efforts included recruiting nurses, distributing supplies, and assisting in communication between soldiers and their families.

Prevention emerged as a major component of the public health movement when Dr. Louis Pasteur and Robert Koch demonstrated that germs—not God or dirt—cause disease. The "golden age of public health" (1890–1910) included the discovery of causes for typhoid, tuberculosis, and cholera. Personal cleanliness, inoculations, serums, and hygienic laws became the basis of reform, and preventive medicine developed beyond research and lab diagnosis. Preventive medicine included a social focus, with well-organized public health education programs (Trattner, 1999). Today, the Public Health Service is part of the Department of Health and Human Services. It focuses on interventions aimed at disease prevention and health promotion that shape a community's overall profile.

Industrialization and its spread around the world during the 19th and 20th centuries stimulated the problems of communicable disease; these were followed by the difficulties that accompanied epidemics of chronic disease—coronary heart disease, cancer, diabetes, and chronic obstructive lung disease. Public health responded to the

61

| BOX 4.4 | PUBLIC HEALTH SERVICES |

The Public Health Service has a distinguished history that dates back to the late 1700s, when many merchant seamen arrived ill and unattached in American port cities that had little capacity to care for them. In 1798, adopting the British tradition of caring for sick mariners at public expense, Congress enacted a measure, which President John Adams signed into law, that provided for "the temporary relief and maintenance of sick or disabled seamen." The first hospital dedicated to the care of merchant sailors was a building purchased near Norfolk, Virginia, in 1801. The first public hospital actually built with tax revenues, however, was in Boston.

Since that time, almost 200 years ago, the Public Health Service has grown to prominence as a federal enterprise dedicated to promoting and protecting the public's health, with a mandate that often embroils its agencies in controversy. The eight agencies of the Public Health Service are the Agency for Health Care Policy and Research, the Agency for Toxic Substances and Disease Registry, the Centers for Disease Control and Prevention (CDC), the Food and Drug Administration (FDA), the Health Resources and Services Administration, the Indian Health Service, the National Institute of Health (NIH), and the Substance Abuse and Mental Health Services Administration.

Source: From "Health Policy Report: Politics and Public Health," by John K. Iglehart, 1996, *Health Policy Report, 334*, p. 203.

first set of problems and has made strides toward controlling the second. A third group of problems that has emerged in the past two decades consists of HIV/AIDS; domestic, school, and street violence; and substance abuse.

Many changes have occurred in public health over the years. In 1789, the Reverend Edward Wigglesworth assessed the health of Americans and produced the first American mortality tables. By 1900, influenza, pneumonia, tuberculosis, and gastrointestinal infections were the main causes of death in the United States. Average life expectancy at birth was 47 years. This last statistic has seen a phenomenal rise, with life expectancy at birth extending to 68 years by 1950, a change attributable to improvements in diet and sanitation and the development of antibiotics and vaccines. By 2004, life expectancy had grown to 77.9 years. Today, leading causes of death are heart disease, cancer, and stroke. The leading health problems are chronic diseases (National Center for Health Life Statistics, 2006).

The Healthy People Initiative, begun in 1979 and reformulated each decade, is the prevention agenda for the United States. It is a national effort to provide a vision for improving the health of all Americans and to guide decisions and actions. Led by the Public Health Service, the initial objectives for 1990 were established in 1980 and expanded for 2000 to include topics such as HIV infection and cancer. Objectives for *Healthy People 2010* were developed through a broad consultation process that involves many different people, states and communities, professional organizations, and other health-oriented groups. Focus areas include chronic kidney disease, disability and secondary conditions, health communication, medical product safety, respiratory diseases, and vision and hearing. You can check the progress of *Healthy People 2010* on its website (http://www.health.gov/healthypeople).

The major challenge has been to shift the national emphasis to prevention, with some of the following successes: Since the 1970s, stroke death rates have declined by 58% and coronary heart disease death rates have declined by 49%; a 32% decline in the death rate from car crashes is attributed to the increased use of safety restraints. Unfortunately, cases of AIDS, tuberculosis, asthma, and birth defects have increased.

TABLE 4.3	SUMMARY POINTS: HISTORY OF THE PUBLIC HEALTH MODEL

- The model fulfills society's interest in assuring healthy conditions.
- Massachusetts Poor Law of 1692 empowered governments to act to promote healthy conditions.
- Local boards of health were established by the end of the 18th century.
- English Public Health Act of 1848 was passed.
- Shattuck (1842) and Chadwick (1850) reports apprised citizens of public health problems.
- The U.S. Sanitary Commission was established in 1861.
- Massachusetts established the first state public health department in 1868.
- By the 1900s, public health adopted a social focus.
- In 1979, the Healthy People Initiative was established.
- *Healthy People 2010* is being implemented.

The Internet has also greatly influenced health care. Health information has proliferated so rapidly that no one knows for certain how many World Wide Web health sites exist. This type of information can be a powerful tool in coping with diseases or maintaining one's health, but oftentimes fast and easy access does not equal accuracy of information. Knowing who puts out the information, checking for frequent updates, and looking for conformity to the Health on the New Foundation's Code of Conduct (HON Code) are clues to the accuracy of information.

CASE STUDIES

The following case study illustrates historical problems that are the primary focus of the public health model. It tells of Sean O'Reilly, who lived in the 1850s in New York City. The study illustrates the living conditions that called attention to public health concerns in America. Especially in larger cities, the problems of immigrants living in poverty greatly challenged public health professionals. The second case study illustrates a major public health effort today.

SEAN O'REILLY

Sean O'Reilly, age 25, was the first member of his family to emigrate from Ireland to America. He joined the great numbers of Irish who came to America in the wake of the potato blight that devastated Ireland in the middle of the 1840s. His journey, in a wooden sailing vessel from Liverpool, took 40 days. The voyage was very difficult. Like most poor immigrants, he traveled in steerage, a lower deck below the water line, reserved for third-class passengers. The space was four to six feet high and lined with two berths of wooden bunks. The floor was crowded with baggage, water, and cord wood. The only fresh air for the steerage area came from the hole in the deck for the hatchway.

After the six-week crossing, Sean emerged from steerage looking pale, weak, and 20 pounds lighter than when he started. He had not succumbed to cholera or dysentery,

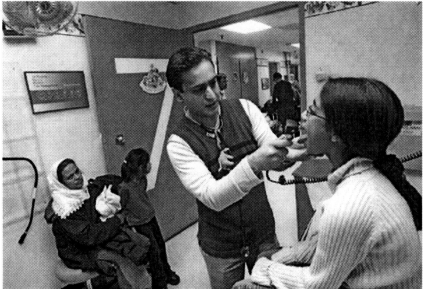

as had several other passengers. The starvation, filth, and crowded conditions he had encountered during the passage to America were just a continuation of the hardships he had experienced in Ireland, which had driven him to emigrate.

The ship docked in New York. Even though Sean did not feel well, he was not eligible for medical treatment from the Marine hospital on Staten Island, as he did not have a communicable disease. Nor did he have enough money to enter Bellevue, the city hospital. He ignored the "runners" who accosted him on board, trying to get him to travel to other cities for a "small" fee. He left the ship and joined hundreds of other new arrivals, mostly Irish like himself, in search of a place to live and a job.

Although Sean had been a farmer in Ireland, he felt that the land had somehow rejected him. He wanted to stay with other Irishmen, near the sea, so he decided to remain in New York City. Sean found work before he found lodging. The first night, he slept in an alley, and the next day he joined a construction gang, moving earth to build roads in the city. The men he met at work suggested that he live with them in a tenement building that housed other newly arrived Irish immigrants. His first Saturday night in America, he was invited to and attended a "kitchen racquet" (get-acquainted party) organized by the family who lived downstairs.

Housing was the most difficult problem Sean faced; laborers' jobs, the sort of work he could do, were plentiful but irregular. Slum lords who took advantage of immigrants in dire need of housing crowded families into small, filthy, dimly lit, poorly ventilated tenements situated on narrow, unpaved streets with inadequate drainage. Partly because there was no integrated health program or municipal board of health, the city was disorderly, dirty, and disease ridden.

From the time he landed, Sean became part of the considerable Irish community in New York. He shared two rooms with a family of six. His living conditions never significantly improved. He held several jobs constructing roads, buildings, and sewage ditches. The jobs involved long hours, hazardous working conditions, low wages, and frequent short periods of unemployment.

Any money he made beyond bare living expenses went to the church and to his small account in the Emigrant Industrial Savings Bank of New York. This account enabled him to bring his family to America through the system known as "one bringing another," in which each immigrant worked and saved for a prepaid ticket for the next member of his family to come to America. By the late 1850s, most of Sean's family had joined him in New York.

REMOTE AREA MEDICAL VOLUNTEER CORPS

Remote Area Medical (RAM) Volunteer Corps is a charitable organization with no paid employees, which uses an airborne force of volunteers dedicated to serving mankind and providing free health care, veterinary services, and technical and educational assistance in remote and rural areas in the United States and around the world. Its history is deeply rooted in the adventuresome nature of its dreamer, designer, and founder, Stan Brock. He lived for many years in the Amazon region of Guyana, South America, where he managed the world's largest tropical ranch. The only medical care was many days' walk away in Georgetown, the nearest city. After ranch owners acquired a small aircraft, he would transport sick or injured people and fly in basic medical necessities. He became a sort of "jungle quack," doing his best to get aid to the rain forest dwellers. When he left there to co-host the Wild Kingdom television series, he traveled extensively, still discovering people who were medically helpless all over the world. He vowed that some day he would find a way to take medical care to people who had none.

The vow became reality when RAM was incorporated in March 1985 and subsequently received tax-exempt charity status by the Internal Revenue Service. Since then, there have been as many as 34 yearly expeditions, serving thousands of people and animals on a conservative budget amounting to over $7.5 million. There is a medical record on every person and animal treated.

RAM has used the services of over 3,500 volunteers from throughout the United States, Canada, Europe, and South America. RAM volunteer health care delivery teams consist of physicians and surgeons of all specialties, nurses, dentists, dental assistants, optometrists, opticians, technicians, veterinarians, and administrative and logistical support personnel who travel to destinations as far away as India or who work here in the United States. Team members pay their own expenses and are asked to procure medicines and other supplies. A team might have as few as 10 members or as many as 40.

RAM teams go only where they are invited. Word of mouth, an expedition nearby, a news article, and often unknown sources familiarize a group or community with its services and frequently generate invitations. The team carefully assesses the area's needs, visits the site, and when appropriate, arranges an expedition. In addition to activity in this country, RAM has programs underway in Guatemala, Haiti/Dominican Republic, India, and South America. Foreign expeditions can be ten days to three weeks in length, during which team members might treat as many as 4,000 patients.

RAM medical services run the gamut from a basic blood pressure check to full scale surgery. Operating teams repair cleft lips and palates, remove cataracts, correct eye muscle problems, and perform trauma surgical procedures. Internal medicine, family practice, or emergency specialists provide treatment for skin disorders, intestinal parasites, tropical diseases, and routine ailments and injuries. Dental teams offer emergency extractions and restorative work. Eye care professionals check visual acuity, examine for ocular disease, and dispense free eyeglasses. Thousands of pairs of eyeglasses a year are secured from the Lions Club Eyeglass Recycling program and

65

carried overseas. In this country, RAM's portable optical lab enables skilled technicians to make new glasses to prescription on site. All providers strive to educate patients, their family members, and the community about the basics of oral and physical health, first aid, hygiene, food handling, clean water, animal management, and self-care.

Remote Area Medical is unique in the scope of services it offers, the frequency with which teams are dispatched, its local and international focus, the variety of destinations selected yearly, and the success of its multifaceted mission. It is truly a relief organization by people of the world for people of the world.

The following questions will help you clarify the role of public health today.

- How do the public health problems in the last case study compare with those Sean O'Reilly encountered?
- How do these two case studies illustrate what you have read about the history of the public health model?
- How do the solutions in public health in the 1850s differ from those today?

THE HUMAN SERVICE MODEL

DEFINITION

A primary focus of the human service model is to provide services that help individuals solve their problems. As Table 4.4 shows, this model differs considerably from the medical model and the public health model. According to the human service model, problems are an expected and even necessary part of everyday life. They occur because human existence is a complex process, involving interaction with other individuals, groups, institutions, and the environment. The human service model considers the problem of the individual within the context of the environment. If an individual must be temporarily removed from the environment to provide effective treatment, then treatment within the context of the environment will continue once the individual reenters that environment.

Individuals are one of the *clients* or *consumers* of the human service system. Clients can include smaller groups such as families, larger geographic populations such as neighborhoods or communities, and populations having problems in common such as the homeless and substance abusers.

The primary method of treatment or service is **problem solving,** a process focused on the here and now that maximizes the identification and use of client strengths. The first phase, problem identification, is critical to the entire process. Correctly identifying the problem, be it uncontrollable anger, unemployment, chronic tardiness, housing, or substance abuse, for example, focuses the process on resolution. Incorrectly identifying the problem may result in client frustration, the perception of the helper as ineffective, and a continuing problem. For these reasons, human service professionals take time to build a relationship with their clients, fully explore the problem or situation that the client is experiencing, and identify any strengths or resources that the client may have.

Once the problem is accurately identified and client strengths determined, some type of intervention may occur. The goal of the intervention varies depending on

TABLE 4.4 | AN OVERVIEW OF THREE MODELS OF SERVICE DELIVERY

	View of the problem	Who is the client?	Who is the worker?	Where does the treatment occur?	Method of treatment	Goal of treatment
Medical	Individual has a physiologically based illness or disease	Individual who receives services is called *patient*	Trained professional in health sciences (physician, nurse, dentist, psychiatrist)	Office Institution	Diagnosis Treatment Behavioral prescription Medication Psychoanalysis	Return individual to prior state
Public Health	Individual, groups, and society have disease or illness. Environmental and social pressures also contribute to problem.	Individuals and special populations or geographic areas (community, neighborhood, state, nation) can be clients	Public health training combines medical knowledge with community action skills	Office Community	Medical diagnosis Prescription Education Mobilization of resources Advocacy for special populations	Prevention Social action
Human Services	"Problems in living" may be internal, environmental, and/or intrapersonal	Individuals, families, special populations, and environment can be clients	Volunteer Paraprofessional Entry-level human worker who works with abuse, rehabilitation, education, etc. Professionals (rehabilitation or mental health counselor, social worker, psychologist)	Offices/agencies/ institutions serving individuals, families, children Community	Problem-solving process	Enhance client's well-being, quality of life Teach client problem-solving skills Prevention

67

the problem. Generally, problems occur in one or more of three areas: emotions, thoughts or beliefs, and behaviors. Problems that deal with feelings or emotions such as feeling inferior or lacking self-awareness may respond best to strategies that encourage the verbal and nonverbal expressions of feelings or sensory imaging (Okun, 2002). If problems relate to how one thinks, for example, solving problems or interpreting situations, then learning coping skills, reframing, or restructuring may be helpful. Violence, a habit like smoking, and self-defeating actions are examples of behavioral problems that may respond to strategies such as reinforcement, contracts, and homework assignments. More complex problems like eating disorders, phobias, and depression may be a combination of all three areas and consequently, require an intervention that addresses all areas.

Identifying strengths follows the same process of enumerating emotions, thoughts, or beliefs and behaviors that have helped the clients succeed in the past. The client is encouraged to match personal strengths to identified problems as a way of planning interventions.

The problem-solving approach is used in this model for several reasons. First, the process provides a systematic way of thinking about complex situations. Problem identification suggests ways to describe situations in clear, understandable terms, encouraging the client and the worker to prioritize the problems that need to be addressed and discouraging impulsive, reactive behaviors. As a part of this approach, client strengths focus on the positive rather than deficits, an encouraging approach for clients. Second, the effectiveness of the process can be assessed at each stage. If the worker or the client discovers new information or if the problem or the environment changes, then the process can be revised. Third, clients can learn this problem-solving process and use it themselves when they no longer require services. Clients have the opportunity to improve their own problem-solving skills by working with a human service worker to solve problems and by rehearsing the behaviors under the worker's direction. Fourth, the outcomes of the process support the philosophy of human services by fostering client self-esteem and sense of personal responsibility as clients work successfully through the process. In addition, the results of the process improve the quality of life for the client. Fifth, the approach is a tool for identifying other problems that may occur and determining strategies to prevent future problems.

PHILOSOPHY

In its broadest sense, the philosophy of human services was solidified during the 1940s. It included the following beliefs:

- People had the right to expect their society, through its technology and other resources, to prevent their deprivation and provide for their basic human needs.
- The society, through its government, had the irrevocable responsibility for providing people with adequate human services.

The community health movement, directly related to deinstitutionalization contributed to the development of a human service model. Community mental health centers often were modeled after other public health efforts. Bringing services to those

TABLE 4.5	SUMMARY POINTS: THE PROBLEM-SOLVING PROCESS

- Process focuses on here and now
- Phases or steps range from three to six
- Process begins with problem identification and identifying client strengths
- Process then moves to decision-making stage
- Process terminates in implementation
- Evaluation is important throughout the process
- Meeting people's needs comprehensively and effectively requires an understanding of the "whole person" and his [or her] relationship to [the] environment
- Meeting the "whole person's" needs means that the resources of many disciplines should be cooperatively mobilized for him [or her]

Source: Adapted from *Human Services Today*, by K. Eriksen, p. 53. Copyright © 1981 by Reston Publishing.

in need within the framework of community health helped broaden the definitions of care, services, recipients, and goals of intervention. At about the same time the medical field began to recognize of the goals of the human service field. The medical profession began stressing patient responsibility for diet, exercise, recreation, and rest. A third factor contributing to the growth of the human service model was the support of President Jimmy Carter, who publicized the fact that Americans did not have access to adequate mental health care. This was attributed to residence, gender, race, and age. Carter's understanding of the mental health dilemma reflects the human service philosophy of the 1940s, with its emphasis on both the responsibilities of society and the importance of working with the whole person.

Most authors agree that a model of human service delivery should include the following characteristics or themes (Burger & Youkeles, 2004; Eriksen, 1981; Harris, Maloney, & Rother, 2004; Mehr & Kanwischer, 2004):

1. The **generic focus** is critical in both human service training and delivery.
2. Services should be accessible, comprehensive, and coordinated.
3. The *problem-solving approach* emphasizes the here and now. Included in this approach are the acts of helping the client solve the problem and teaching the client problem-solving skills while building on client strengths.
4. Taking into consideration the impact of social institutions, social systems, and social problems, the model works with the person and the environment.

TABLE 4.6	SUMMARY POINTS: HISTORY OF THE HUMAN SERVICE MODEL

- 1940s—Development of human service philosophy occurs.
- 1950–1990—Community mental health movement expands definition of "good care."
- 1960s—Medical profession recognizes importance of human service goals.
- 1990s—Human service educators recognize common human service themes.

5. Treating the *whole* person is best accomplished when the worker recognizes client needs in relation to others and to the environment.
6. Human services is *accountable to the consumer*. Clients are active participants in the human service model, making decisions, taking action, and accepting responsibility for themselves.

CASE STUDY

The following case study illustrates several concepts you have read about in this chapter. It presents four possible clients who are experiencing problems and who have different perspectives on their problems. This situation also illustrates both the individual and the family as clients. Let us focus first on the human service model of service delivery.

Consider yourself the human service professional who has received the following case. As you read it, think about these questions:

*   How have Susan, Ted, Justin, and Matthew solved problems in the past?
*   How do you think each person in the case study will define the problems?
*   As you consider problem solving as a systematic way of thinking, how would you as a human service professional approach the problem Susan faces?
*   Identify any strengths of any of the four individuals that might be helpful in addressing problems.
*   How will the themes and characteristics of human services guide your work with this case?

SUSAN AND TED

Susan and Ted met in college, where she was studying to be a teacher and he was studying to be an engineer. Ted was from an upper-middle-class family; Susan, from a religious, working-class family. Even while they were dating, Ted was a heavy "social drinker," but Susan ignored his drinking. She wanted to marry a man with a college education and have a large family. She came from a small, close-knit family and had only one sister. She remembered her family as having few luxuries while she was growing up, but much love and nurturance. Ted's family was also small, but not close. Ted had no contact with his family, even though they lived in the same town as the university.

During Ted and Susan's sophomore year, Susan's grades began to fall. She was on a partial scholarship and was in danger of losing it. She dropped out of school and moved out of the dorm into an apartment with Ted. Then Susan became pregnant. Ted dropped out of school and got a job as a draftsperson for a small local firm. They married.

Leaving behind a happy, carefree life without responsibility, they now faced an uncertain future. Susan tried to be the "perfect wife" her mother had been. She was determined to work before the baby was born and assume the role of homemaker. Ted began drinking heavily. He lost several jobs during Susan's pregnancy and often took his anger out on her by hitting her and keeping her constantly tense and fearful. He turned to drugs, and the relationship deteriorated further.

After losing several more jobs, Ted had to take a menial, low-paying job just to make ends meet, and his resentment increased. He spent more time away from home, leaving Susan with only the money she was earning for food or transportation.

70

She was alone and depressed but did not confide in her family, because she did not want to upset them.

Often Ted was away for days. As Susan's pregnancy progressed, he became more violent. Once, he beat her so badly that he cracked two of her ribs and broke her nose. He also attempted to strangle her. She told no one and lied to her doctor, coworker, and friends about the injuries. Ted "came to his senses" and tried to make amends, but he began drinking heavily once again and in a fit of rage kicked her in the stomach, bringing on labor. Susan delivered a son in the sixth month of her pregnancy. Justin weighed 3 pounds, 2 ounces, and had difficulty breathing. He was placed in an intensive-care nursery for six weeks before his parents could take him home. During this time, Susan worked and Justin continued to be sickly, suffering from chronic ear infections and colic. Ted had trouble adjusting to his new son, so Susan quit her job and took care of him alone.

Justin had many health problems and was constantly under the care of physicians. He was often hospitalized with pneumonia and severe dehydration. When Justin was 14 months old, Ted deserted them. Susan had no money, no job, and no car. She turned to her parents for a small loan and got a job in a department store making minimum wage. She had to work, but it angered her to leave Justin with a babysitter. Being a single parent was difficult. By the time she paid the rent, the bills, and the babysitter, there was no money left. She was desperately unhappy but determined to make the best of things.

Several months later, Ted returned. He had a new job making good money and was ready to "work things out." He continued to drink and he still beat her, but she now wanted him at any cost. He soon learned this fact. One year later, Susan had another son, Matthew. At this point, Ted and Susan bought a house in a small town near the university and proceeded to raise their family. For Ted, this consisted of nightly bouts with the bottle in front of a television set and of forcing himself sexually on Susan. The years passed, and Susan continued to put up with his drinking and rapes. Eventually, Ted's drinking became uncontrollable, and he started abusing the children.

One night he came home late, pulled a gun, and shot at Susan. A neighbor called the police; he was handcuffed and arrested. Ted's father, who had previously been completely out of the picture, now came to Ted's aid by paying his bail. This became a regular routine. Each time Ted was out of jail, he would return home to drink and terrorize Susan and the children. After six months, Susan told Ted she wanted a divorce. He became enraged and threatened her. She persisted and engaged a lawyer.

Her intention was to return to the university to finish her education and continue with her plans to be a teacher. She had less than two years to go and was confident that with child support, income from a job, and financial aid, this plan was feasible. Until the divorce, Ted refused to leave the house. The boys suffered terribly, seeing their mother beaten and their father handcuffed and taken to jail in a police car.

Currently, the youngest child, Matthew, now 14, works part time while attending high school as a sophomore. He is doing poorly in school but is managing to pass his courses. He likes his job and the money he makes. He is able to help pay for some of the things the family needs. He no longer has plans for college and, indeed, intends to continue working at the pizza restaurant if and when he graduates from high school. Although Matthew's grades have recently dropped from As to Cs and Ds, Justin's grades have suffered the most. He is now failing all his classes and has developed severe behavioral and emotional problems. He skips school, refuses to do his homework, and "hangs out with the wrong crowd." He takes drugs at home and school and sells drugs to his classmates. Justin is extremely depressed and hostile. He carries a knife to school and threatens classmates with it.

71

During one incident, when the victim's parents pressed charges, Justin was suspended from school and referred to the juvenile correctional department. He was placed in a program for adolescents who are dependent on alcohol or drugs. School officials realize that Justin "has problems" but have offered Susan no guidance or support, taking action only when Justin's behavior is life threatening.

Justin received correctional treatment in a private residential hospital, but it took some time to get him into treatment since he was not covered by his father's insurance plan. He had been admitted on his father's insurance card, but two days later the company denied the claim. Susan discovered that she was not covered by Ted's insurance and he refused to add Justin to his policy (he did not tell Susan that he did not have an insurance policy). Susan applied to the state for insurance and was covered after a two-month wait. Justin then entered the hospital and began to improve. Unfortunately, the state coverage limited the stay Justin needed. He remained and Susan is now received bills totaling more than $80,000 that she is expected to pay. She knows she will soon have to admit to the hospital that she cannot pay.

Susan is in trouble financially. She receives free medical aid from the university student clinic. Last Christmas, a church she joined took up a collection for her and the children and bought them $200 worth of groceries. She requested one month of subsidized utilities from the local utilities company but is eligible for this assistance only one time. She is concerned that she will not be able to afford utilities this month. Ted pays child support only sporadically, and he moves from town to town. He pays just enough to satisfy state requirements, so Susan has little legal recourse.

Susan never knows where she can find him in case of an emergency and is not certain he would even help. Ted continues to have visitation rights since visitation is not linked to child support. Susan is furious about this privilege but keeps thinking he will eventually take more responsibility for his children. Constantly depressed because of her situation, Susan also fears that bill collectors will start to hound her and that, if an emergency occurs, she will not be able to handle it. She does not know what to do.

As you think about these clients' needs from the human service perspective, you quickly realize that $200 for groceries and one month of subsidized utilities solve only immediate problems. The larger problems that Susan, Ted, Justin, and Matthew face are much more complex and will require comprehensive, coordinated service delivery.

You have learned in this chapter that human service professionals use three primary models of service delivery. In taking charge of this case, you will function within the context of the human service model. To promote the well-being of the whole person and to provide the comprehensive services necessary to that end, you may rely on professionals whose service delivery is guided by the public health model or by the medical model. To minimize duplication of services and to promote coordinated service delivery, you need to maintain active links with other professionals who may work with the same clients as you do.

Now that you are familiar with the history of Susan, Ted, Matthew, and Justin, review the problem-solving process. Select one of the individuals in the case study as your client and ask yourself the following questions:

- What is the mindset of this client now?
- What problems and subproblems does the client face?
- What alternatives are possible to solve these problems?
- How would you as the helping professional use the human service model in this case?

72

- What services might be provided by professionals who practice the medical model, the public health model, or both?
- How can a human service professional facilitate the interaction of all three models in resolving client problems?

Using models is a helpful way of identifying the different approaches to clients' problems. The distinctions among the models are not arbitrary, for each has a separate history and has developed in response to different social needs. From the human service perspective, however, each model has a part in the problem-solving process. The worker is responsible for blending the models and the treatments or services they represent in response to client needs. Indeed, one strength of human services is the focus on clients' needs and the flexibility to use approaches from various models to meet those needs.

KEY TERMS

antianxiety drugs	electroshock therapy	neurosis	psychoanalytic method
antidepressant drugs	generic focus	patient	psychopharmacology
antipsychotic drugs	human service model	prevention	psychotropic drugs
client	medical model	problem solving	public health model
consumer	mood stabilizers	psychiatry	

THINGS TO REMEMBER

1. Three different models represent orientations in service delivery: the medical model, the public health model, and the human service model.

2. Underlying each of the three models is a set of philosophical assumptions that guide the delivery of services and shape beliefs about the causes of problems, their treatment, and the role of the professional in service delivery.

3. The medical model views the person coming for help as a *patient* whose problem is diagnosed as a disease or sickness and treated by a physician or service provider who prescribes a treatment or cure for the "disease."

4. At the turn of the 20th century, Mary Richmond, author of *Social Diagnosis,* used the medical model to describe social casework.

5. Until the end of the 19th century, insanity was socially defined, but when psychiatry emerged as a medical specialty, insanity became a medical label.

6. Psychotropic drugs are now among the most widely used treatments for mental disorders. Psychopharmacology, the study of the effects of drugs on mental health, is an area of interest to human service professionals.

7. The public health model, like the medical model, focuses on individuals and larger populations; it attempts to solve many of society's social problems.

8. Communicable diseases, poor sanitation, and lack of medical knowledge have been primary community health problems since ancient times. Laws such as the Massachusetts Poor Law of 1692 in North America and the

73

Public Health Act of 1848 in Britain initiated efforts to improve public health conditions.

9. The U.S. Sanitary Commission was the first major public health group in the United States. Its efforts were primarily preventive, alerting the public to the benefits of preventive sanitary measures.

10. A primary focus of the human service model is to provide services that help individuals solve their problems, including a consideration of client problems within the context of their environments.

11. Individuals are among the clients of the human service system, as are small groups, larger geographic populations, populations defined by lifestyle, and populations that have problems in common.

12. The primary method of treatment is problem solving, a process focused on the here and now that encompasses three phases: problem identification, decision making, and problem resolution.

13. The human service philosophy emphasizes both the responsibilities of society and the importance of working with the whole person.

14. Themes characteristic of human service delivery are its generic focus; accessible, integrated services; problem-solving approach; treatment of the whole person; and accountability to the consumer.

15. Using models is a helpful way to identify the different approaches to clients' problems.

ADDITIONAL READINGS: FOCUS ON MENTAL ILLNESS

Karp, D. (2002). *The burden of sympathy: How families cope with mental illness.* NY: Oxford University Press.
The experiences of family members of the mentally ill who have survived provide caregivers aid, guidance, and solace. The similarities of caregiver experiences, the challenge of finding and maintaining equilibrium, and a critical look at what it means to be a moral and caring person come from 60 extensive interviews.

Kotuiski T. (2006). *Saving Millie: A daughter's story of surviving her mother's schizophrenia.* Madelia, MN: Extraordinary Voices Press.
The author recounts her experiences with her mother to serve as a resource for families dealing with schizophrenia and a broken health care system.

Pederson, J. (2004). *The panic diaries: The frightful, sometimes hilarious truth about panic attacks.* Berkeley, CA: Ulysses Press.
The focus of this book is what panic is, how it is experienced, and how it is treated. Interviews with psychiatrists, psychologists, and other health professionals offer suggestions for treatments. Symptoms, treatments, advocacy, and resources add to its comprehensiveness.

Slater, L. (1999). *Prozac diary.* New York: Penguin Books.
Lauren Slater, patient, therapist, and author of *Welcome to My Country*, shares what it is like to be cured by America's preeminent selective serotonin reuptake inhibitor.

Torrey, E. F. (2005). *Surviving manic depression: A manual on bipolar disorder for patients, families, and providers.* NY: Basic Books. This book provides a guide to living with bipolar disorder—symptoms, treatments, and advocacy.

Whitaker, R., & Whitaker, B. (2001). Mad in America: Bad science, bad medicine, and the enduring mistreatment of the mentally ill. Boulder, CO: Perseus Publishing.
Why are the cure rates for schizophrenia so low in America, the most well-developed country in the world? This exposé surveys 300 years of mental health treatments and attitudes.

REFERENCES

Afifi, A., & Breslow, L. (1994). The maturing paradigm of public health. *Annual Review of Public Health, 15,* 223–235.

Burger, W. R., & Youkeles, M. (2004). *Human services in contemporary America* (5th ed.). Pacific Grove, CA: Brooks/Cole/ Thomson Learning.

Clear, T. R., Cole, G. F., Resig, M. D. (2005). *American corrections.* Belmont, CA: Wadsworth/Thomson.

Committee Study of the Future of Public Health Institute of Medicine. (1988). *The future of public health.* Washington, DC: National Academy Press.

Eriksen, K. (1981). *Human services today.* Reston, VA: Reston Publishing.

Hamlin, P. (1985). *Experiences in mental institutions: Case studies.* Unpublished manuscript.

Harris, H. S., Maloney, D. C., & Rother, F. M. (2004). *Human services: Contemporary issues and trends* (3rd ed.). Needham, MA: Allyn & Bacon.

Ingersoll, R. E., & Rak, C. F. (2006). *Psychopharmacology for helping professionals: An integral exploration.* Belmont, CA: Thomson Brooks/Cole.

Mehr, J., & Kanwischer, R. (2004). *Human services: Concepts and intervention strategies* (9th ed.). Boston: Allyn & Bacon.

National Center for Life Health Statistics. (2006). *Life expectancy.* Retrieved August 10, 2006, from http://www.cdc.gov/nchs/fastats/lifexpec.htm.

Okun, B. F. (2002). *Effective helping: Interviewing and counseling techniques* (6th ed.). Pacific Grove, CA: Brooks/Cole.

Pichot, P. (1985). Remedicalisation of psychiatry. *Psychiatrial Fennica, 16,* 9–17.

Reinhard, S. (1986). Financing long-term health care of the elderly: Dismantling the medical model. *Public Health Nursing, 3*(1), 3–22.

Richmond, M. (1917). *Social diagnosis.* New York: Sage.

Seligman, M. (2004). *Authentic happiness: Using the new positive psychology to realize your potential for lasting fulfillment.* New York: Free Press.

Shirreffs, J. H. (1982). *Community health: Contemporary perspectives.* Englewood Cliffs, NJ: Prentice Hall.

Spake, A. (2003, September 15). Public health. *U.S. News and World Report, 135*(8), 30.

Trattner, W. I. (1999). *From poor law to welfare state: A history of social welfare in America.* New York: Free Press.

Zimbalist, S. E. (1977). *Historic themes and landmarks in social welfare research.* New York: Harper & Row.

CHAPTER 8 | WORKING WITHIN A SYSTEM

After reading this chapter, you will be able to:

- Describe the agency environment.
- Use the referral process.
- Build an information network.
- Identify the challenges in day-to-day human services.
- Define encapsulation and burnout in human services.
- Describe methods of promoting change.

Self-assessment

- Identify ways the professional can learn more about an agency.
- Explain the steps you would use to decide when to refer.
- What is a "good" referral?
- Describe the challenges the human service professional faces.
- How can professional development counter these challenges?
- How can human service professionals promote change?
- What are the pitfalls a professional may encounter while developing services in response to community needs?
- Why is the client empowerment model for change an effective one?

Many human services are provided within the context of an agency or organization in a community or a geographic area. This context or environment for human service delivery is important to those who work within its structure and boundaries. It would be difficult to assist clients, to deliver effective services, and to develop needed policies and services without an understanding of this context. This chapter will introduce the concept of the human service environment and its integral role in the work of human service professionals.

Agencies and organizations set the parameters or boundaries of the work of their employees. Concepts such as mission, structure, funding, and resources influence the world of human service agencies and organizations. Because agencies and organizations do not function in a vacuum, this chapter then introduces the larger environment of the community to help us understand the context in which the agency operates. Knowledge of the available resources in a community is part of the larger context. Some of the daily challenges encountered by human service professionals are also explored. Agencies and communities are dynamic, constantly shifting in response to social, political, and economic change. The chapter concludes with a look at ways in which the human service professional can facilitate change.

THE AGENCY ENVIRONMENT

The world of the human service agency is a complex one. In fact, when we talk about an agency's purpose or structure, it may almost seem like we are using another language. The purpose of this next section is to introduce the concepts that help define an agency. Understanding these concepts will increase your knowledge of human service delivery and the environment in which it occurs.

MISSION AND GOALS

One of the first questions you may have upon learning about an agency is "What does this agency do?" Several agency documents provide answers to this question. The first document is the agency's written **mission**. This is a statement that communicates the purpose of the agency by summarizing its guiding principles. Generally, it is relatively brief and appears in a prominent place at the agency, such as the entrance or reception area. It is usually included in all agency publications. A mission statement may identify the population served, the broad goals of the agency, sources of funding, the values that influence decision making, the agency structure, and agency priorities (Lewis, Lewis, Packard, & Souflee, 2006). It is also an important source of information about an agency's function and direction. An example of a mission statement is that of Aging with Dignity: "Our mission is to help you and your family plan and receive the care you deserve" (Aging with Dignity, 2006).

Other documents shed light on the work of an agency by clarifying rules and regulations, the work of the staff, and the standards of practice. These documents include goal statements, job descriptions, and policies and procedures. An example of a goal statement might read like this one from the Social Support Center in Abu Dhabi, United Arab Emirates: "Our goal: A Community without Crimes, A Stable Family, and A Safe Individual" (Social Support Center, 2006). To achieve this goal, Social Support Center Staff are guided by the following principles:

- Respect for human right and dignity of families and individuals
- Preservation and prevalence of law
- Keeping work as well as the parties related to the cases confidential
- Showing initiative and promptness in response, and fruitful work without limits
- Cooperation and coordination with various related parties and institutions, in order to ensure that all concerned categories are being supported
- To be wise and patient, and to discuss and consider carefully before making decisions (Social Support Center, 2006).

Another way to learn about an agency is by reading information about its job openings. When you apply for a position in a human service agency, the first exposure you will have to that position is the advertisement. Generally, it will include a brief job description, the qualifications, and sometimes a salary range or a statement that "salary is commensurate with experience." As you read the following position announcements, think about the questions you would ask if you were applying for one of these jobs.

Respite Counselor—Bachelor's degree in child development, human services, or related field. Minimum of one year experience working with children, youth, and families, and referral sources; good interpersonal skills working with seriously emotionally disturbed youth; flexible hours with occasional weekend work; some travel within a three-county region. Driver's license and safe driving record required.

Case Manager—Provide counseling, prevention services, mentoring, and case management services to adolescents in the community; facilitate parent and adolescent support groups; maintain accurate case records and reports; link youth and families to appropriate community resources; other duties as assigned. Qualifications: High school diploma or GED and five years experience working with youth and families; Associate's degree preferred and previous experience working with abuse, neglect, and special needs.

Children and Youth Crisis Treatment Team Member—Bachelor's degree in social sciences and one year professional experience working with children and youth preferred. Provide intensive case management services to mentally ill children, adolescents, and their families; work as part of a multidisciplinary team; position requires some flexibility with schedule.

If you want to learn more about a job, one request you might make is to read the official **job description** of the position. This is a written document that defines the duties and responsibilities and is much more extensive than a brief job announcement. For example, it lists the expectations for the person in the position, the job qualifications, and a salary range. Unfortunately, job descriptions are often general in nature, rarely capturing the realities of the day-to-day work. A job description may also change as a result of reorganization, changing client needs, and economic pressures. Still, it remains an important document that offers guidelines about agency expectations. The job description in Box 8.1 is for the case management position advertised. This position is with a nonprofit agency that serves children and families. As you read this job description, what additional information do you now have about the position? What else would you like to know?

Another source of important information is the policies and procedures that guide the work of the agency. An agency policy might detail how its governing board is selected or who the agency accepts for services. The school you are attending has policies about the number of hours you can take each term. An agency procedure reflects accepted standards of practice. For example, the steps necessary to spend agency funds for a client service or the rules regarding the release of client information provide a guide for the human service professional to do his or her job. Procedures at your school tell you how to register for courses or how to withdraw from school. It is important to be familiar with all policies and procedures.

Policies and procedures also influence the **organizational climate** of an agency. This term refers to the conditions of the work environment that affect how people experience their work. The range of responsibility and decision making and the intensity and frequency of supervision are examples of factors that contribute to the organizational climate. For example, is the human service professional free to determine his or her work schedule, make final recommendations for client treatment, or authorize expenditures for client services?

STRUCTURE

Another way to understand a human service agency is to learn about the way it is organized. This is the structure of the agency, and it refers to the relationships among the people who work there and the departments to which they are assigned. There are two helpful concepts that illustrate the structure of an agency. One is the **chain of command.** This refers to the layers of authority in an agency. For example, those at the

80

| BOX 8.1 | HELP WANTED: A CASE MANAGER |

CHILD AND FAMILY SERVICES
Job Description

POSITION TITLE: Case Manager
Program: PARTNERS Teen Pregnancy and Responsible Parents

Effective Date: April 1

POSITION OBJECTIVE:

To provide case management services to adolescents, their families, and noncustodial parents. Case managers are advocates for customers and focus on goals that will move participants toward self-sufficiency.

ESSENTIAL FUNCTIONS:

- Provide counseling, mentoring, and case management services to adolescents
- Emphasize the importance of self-sufficiency to youth and responsibility to all parents
- Provide prevention services to youth in the community
- Facilitate parent and adolescent support groups
- Establish and maintain accurate case records and reports
- Link youth and families to appropriate community resources
- Assist with community presentations
- Assist noncustodial parents, youth, and their families with any barrier that they feel is preventing progress
- Monitor attendance and measure progress

- Maintain regular and predictable job attendance
- Work cooperatively with coworkers and residents
- Other duties as assigned

This list of essential functions is not intended to be exhaustive. Child & Family Services reserves the right to revise this job description as needed to comply with actual job requirements.

QUALIFICATIONS:

Required:

- High school diploma or GED
- Five years experience working with youth and families

Preferred:

- Associate's degree in social services—related field
- Previous experience working with abuse, neglect, and/or special needs children and their families

top of the chain control resources and actions. Lines of authority emanate from the top in most agencies. For some agencies, the chain of command is hierarchical with defined responsibilities and accountability from top to bottom. Each person is accountable for those under his or her supervision. Other agencies have a flatter chain of command. This means that there are fewer layers of authority from top to bottom so that decision making is more of a shared responsibility.

A second concept that is helpful in understanding the structure of an agency is a diagram known as an **organizational chart**. See Figure 8.1. At a glance, it is easy to see the boxes that represent offices, departments, and sometimes individuals. The organizational chart also illustrates the chain of command. The solid lines that connect the boxes clearly show lines of authority, information flow, and accountability. Often, lines connect vertically to represent departments or individuals that work closely together. The boxes identify different services and represent staff dedicated to providing those services.

81

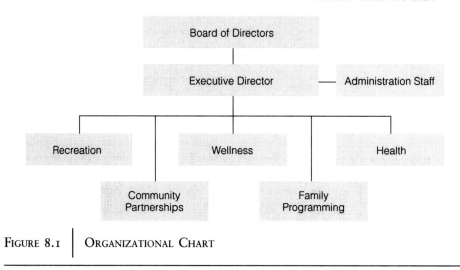

FIGURE 8.1 | ORGANIZATIONAL CHART

RESOURCES

Another source of information about an agency is its funding sources. These determine if an agency is public or governmental, not-for-profit (voluntary), or for-profit. The distinction between public and not-for-profit agencies is not always clear because not-for-profit agencies are increasingly providing services for public agencies on a contractual basis. The number of for-profit agencies is also increasing due to limited resources for voluntary agencies, reduced governmental spending, and changing political and economic times.

The term *revenue* refers to the money an agency receives from four primary sources of funding: federal, state, and local governments; grants and contracts; fees; and donations. It is not unusual for an agency to receive money from multiple sources. Public or governmental agencies receive funding from the federal, state, regional, county, and municipal governments. State government agencies such as a department of human services or a department of family and children are examples. Not-for-profit agencies such as the Red Cross and the Children's Defense Fund are funded by individual contributions, fund-raisers, foundation grants, and corporate donations. For-profit agencies are supported by contracts and fees. In some states, the prison system is run by an agency or organization for profit. This arrangement is often referred to as **privatization.**

These concepts are important in order to understand the context in which human services are delivered. They help human service professionals better understand their job responsibilities and how those responsibilities relate to the agency's mission and goals. They also allow human service professionals who operate within agency policies and procedures to provide effectively and efficiently the services their clients need. Finally, much of the planning and service delivery within an agency relates to funding. Staffing, the number of clients served, and the programs and services provided relate directly to funding.

Agencies have a number of other **resources** to use to develop services and provide them to clients. These resources include the obvious ones, such as available funds, buildings, land, staff, and short-term goods like equipment and supplies. An agency can also use resources that are not so apparent at first glance. One example is the skills and talents of the employees of the organization. These include artistic ability, physical strength, creativity, fund-raising ability, and a talent for advocacy. The skills and talents of patrons of the organization or individuals who volunteer also count as resources. Finding new resources to support agency work helps expand what the agency can do or balances deficits in funding. Homan (2004) suggests that new community resources may be identified by focusing on several aspects of those resources such as identifying major institutions, relevant community information, and personal connection to resources. Resources have a broader meaning than just staff, budget, and buildings. They include institutions, personal talents, relationships, and influences.

THE COMMUNITY CONTEXT

Just as human service professionals operate within the context of an agency or organization, human service agencies exist within the context of a larger framework—the community. For some agencies this may be a housing project or a neighborhood or a county; for other agencies, like state departments of human services or children's services, the community may be an entire state. Whatever the context, studying this larger framework is another way to understand the complexities of human service delivery.

The environments within which agencies exist influence the way they operate, the services provided, the clients served, and the professionals employed. The shared values of the community also influence the agency. The community environment may include other agencies, institutions, the specific missions and philosophies that guide their service delivery, and the specific needs that they address. Other influences include how individuals within these organizations communicate formally and informally with each other.

Community mapping is a strategy that human service professionals and the agencies they represent use to learn about other professionals and agencies. This strategy helps them connect their agencies to the life of the community and its citizens. The people employed by an agency may not be like the clients with whom they work—economically, racially, or ethnically. Yet their clients and the communities in which they live form a critical part of the helper's knowledge base.

How do agencies and their staffs connect with a community? The effective human service agency and its employees will become part of the communities where they are located. This means offering services within the context of client-identified needs; anticipating reactions to differences in race, ethnicity, attitudes, and roles represented by human service professionals; and planning for interactions among clients and helpers. Agencies accomplish this connection in several ways. Some choose to have clients represented on their governing boards or they appoint an advisory committee of clients. Locating the agency within the community is another strategy.

Youth-In-Need, the community organization you read about in Chapter 3, provides support for other agencies with whom it works and has become part of the larger community. Staff work with clients within the community, especially with teens who are homeless. Many staff spend their workdays meeting children and youth

TABLE 8.1	SUMMARY POINTS: AGENCY TERMS

- The brief mission statement of an agency communicates its purpose by summarizing its guiding principles.
- A job description is a written document that defines the duties and responsibilities of a particular position.
- The chain of command in an agency refers to the layers of authority.
- An organizational chart is a diagram that illustrates agency structure.
- Funding sources determine if an agency is public or governmental, not-for-profit, or for-profit.
- Human service agencies exist within the context of a community that influences operations, services, clients, and professionals.

on street corners, alleyways, and other street locations. Other agencies also meet clients where they are: home visits to residences in housing projects; intake interviews under bridges, at shelters, or wherever the homeless are found; meetings at residential centers or institutions for substance abuse, education, or mental illness; or even appointments at local fast-food restaurants.

Interacting in the community with residents, clients, and other professionals is another way that agencies connect with the community. This interaction serves two purposes. The first is to make connections; effective human service professionals who know the community know its resources. These include other human service agencies, religious organizations, service clubs, and businesses. And knowing these resources is the first step toward tapping them. The second purpose is to document the strengths of the community. What are the assets of the community? How can the agency support those assets in order to strengthen the community? How can these strengths be used to attack the problems?

Becoming a part of the community they serve should be the goal of human service agencies. However, the work is not over once this is accomplished. Remaining a part of the community requires continuity and interaction. The process is ongoing.

USING AVAILABLE SERVICES

An important part of the human service professional's responsibility is to work within the larger context of the human service delivery system and the client's environment. Knowledge of both agency and community resources is critical to fulfilling this responsibility. To facilitate this work, the professional will benefit from an understanding of the referral process and related issues.

Referral relates directly to the interaction between the human service professional and the environment by making use of the human service network during the referral process. In seeking services for a client, the helper often relies on other professionals both within and outside the agency to locate the needed services, negotiate introductions and meeting times, and establish the groundwork for the client to visit another

84

agency. A successful referral results in the delivery of the services needed. The referral process is described in this section. The nature of and relationships among agencies and human service professionals contribute to the success of the referral.

REFERRAL

One of the most important roles of a human service professional is **brokering,** or referring a client to another agency or service. The actual referral involves a two-step process: (1) assessing the client's problems and needs, and (2) providing the link between the client and the needed service. To understand the process of referral, the worker must know when to refer, how to refer, where to refer, and how to develop the referral. Successful brokering requires considerable time and skill. Effective referral occurs when the referring professional knows what the clients may expect from another agency; it also helps the referral process if the professional has developed a cooperative relationship with other agency personnel. The human service professional and the client need to understand the services that are provided by the agency or the worker who is receiving the referral; it is important that their expectations match. Cooperation is another key ingredient in an effective referral. All the helpers involved must keep the client's needs as the primary focus. If difficulties arise, they need to remember that the goal is to serve the client well.

To make a successful referral, the helper must have information about a service or agency. This includes its history, possible legislation that affects it, its purpose or intent, and the specific client services it provides. Once the helper has this information, then an assessment begins to determine if the agency meets client needs. Several considerations about the agency need to be considered by the helper. The following questions may assist the helper determine if the agency under consideration is the correct one for the client.

- Will this agency be able to provide the service that the client needs?
- Does this agency accept referrals from us? Do we have a memorandum of agreement or an informal linkage?
- Is the client going to be able to travel to the agency's location?
- Is the intake process simple or streamlined?
- Are the eligibility standards difficult to meet?

In other words, if the services exist but are not readily available to your clients, the agency is not a good referral source.

WHEN TO REFER   A human service professional may send a client to another professional for several reasons. The referral may be client initiated—that is, the client may request a referral. The client may realize that other services would be helpful and thus suggests a specific referral. The client may request that the referral come from the worker in order to give the client more credibility with the new service, speed up the response, or both. In another case, the client may have come to the helper specifically to ask for help in working with other agencies.

Referral may also be appropriate because the helper is not able to provide the assistance necessary to solve the client's problems. The client may present requests or have problems that the worker cannot solve, or the worker may discover that the client has a major problem that must be addressed before the others can be solved and that requires more specialized assistance than the worker can provide. Another reason for referral is that the client may be in serious psychological distress—suicidal or violent— and require intensive therapy or crisis intervention that the worker cannot provide in the human services setting. The helper may also decide to refer the client because of lack of success with that particular client; a different professional would perhaps be more effective.

There are also reasons to consider what might make a referral difficult for the client. The client must want to be referred and be willing to accept services from another source. Second, the client must able to negotiate another agency setting and provide and receive information. If the client is ambivalent about the referral, then the helper must assess if the client can follow-up of his or her own.

How to Refer   Once the helper has decided that the client needs to be referred, the complex process of referral begins. A key word in the referral process is *communication*. The following four-step process provides guidelines for linking the client with another service.

1. *Explain.* The client needs to understand why the referral is taking place. Even if the client initiates the referral, the client must understand that he or she is not just being passed on to the next human service professional. Referral is a thoughtful activity, initiated for the good of the client.
2. *Describe the services.* The client needs to be informed about the referral agency and its services. The more information the worker can give about the intake process, the services available, the fee structure, and the professionals in the agency, the more comfortable the client will be in making the initial contact.
3. *Know the contact.* Talk to the agency and get the name of the contact person, the telephone number, the address, and directions to the agency. Help the client make the appointment for the initial visit to the agency.
4. *Transmit information.* Send appropriate information about the client to the new service, always considering what that agency needs to know about the client. This will allow the agency to plan. Sometimes information can be sent electronically, which speeds up the flow of information.

Where to Refer   To determine where to refer the client, the human service professional must first identify the client's problems. Then the worker must find services to meet those needs. The worker may use services that are familiar or may investigate other possibilities. Both formal and informal networks (described later in this chapter) are useful in determining what services are available and appropriate to meet the client's needs.

Home health services, a popular alternative today to hospitalization, depend on referral resources. The goals of these services are increasing client independence and minimizing the limitations of illness or disability. In many cases, this means knowing where needed services and products can be located. Home Health Source is an example of this community-based service (see Box 8.2).

86

| BOX 8.2 | HOME HEALTH SERVICES |

According to the Bureau of Labor Statistics (2006), home health care services include skilled nursing care or medical services, primarily to the elderly, in the home of the patient. This service was created for dual purposes, to provide care to those who can not travel to care centers and to save financial resources. This was once a small component of the health care system, but its use and availability is increasing rapidly (Bureau of Labor Statistics).

Home health care services today include in-home nursing care, rehabilitation and therapy following hospitalization. They also includes assistance in daily living for those who can not provide care to themselves. Specific services include orthopedic-related treatment, fall-related assessment and treatment, cardiopulmonary disease management, rehabilitation services for traumatic brain injury and spinal chord injury, respiratory therapy, hospice, and consultation.

EVALUATING THE REFERRAL   The referral process does not end once the referral has been made; it continues with systematic follow-up. The helper can call the agency to learn whether the client has kept the appointment and can call the client to get the client's evaluation of the service. The worker needs to know if the service was effective and if the help received matched the worker's assessment of the problem. Such follow-up can be very time-consuming for the helper but will be valuable not only for this client but also for others in the future. It is especially good feedback for the professional and increases the client's faith in the system. The follow-up also reinforces the professional's care for and commitment to the client.

Making referrals is difficult for several reasons. Agencies are constantly changing, and maintaining an accurate picture of an agency, its current staff, and the services it provides is difficult. Sometimes services are not designed to meet the exact needs of the client, and the referring worker cannot guarantee treatment to the client. Each agency must independently assess the client's needs and the agency's ability to meet those needs. The service may not be provided because the client does not meet the eligibility criteria, because the services needed do not exist, or because there is a waiting list for assistance. The agency may not cooperate fully with the referring agency in the referral process or the follow-up. Many agencies also are so understaffed that they simply do not have the staff to provide follow-up.

BUILDING AN INFORMATION NETWORK

To make successful referrals, the human service professional must make effective use of all the resources in a community. First, the helper must know what services are available. The beginning professional is at a particular disadvantage because of a lack of experience in the system, a lack of personal contacts with other professionals in the system, and a lack of knowledge about the many problems that clients may have. Therefore, the helper must develop a systematic way of building a file of information about the human service network for referral purposes. The worker must first decide how to categorize the information to be gathered. Whether services are being organized by the physical, social, and emotional needs of the clients, the specific populations served, or one of the other organizational frameworks mentioned, the

87

TABLE 8.2 | SUMMARY POINTS: REFERRALS

- The agency to which the client is referred must be able and willing to provide the service, be accessible geographically, and have reasonable eligibility criteria.

- A referral may be appropriate when the professional cannot provide the needed service or when the professional believes another helper might be more effective.

- When referring, the helper explains the purpose of the referral, describes the services, talks with the agency to identify a contact person, and sends appropriate client information to the agency receiving the referral.

- It is necessary to identify the client's problem prior to deciding where to refer.

- Follow-up to evaluate the success of the referral completes the referral process.

---

categories will help the worker think about how services are delivered in the community.

The helper can then begin to collect information and record it using computer software, a Blackberry or other hand held device, a card file, a file box, a loose-leaf notebook, or any other storage device that allows for easy additions and revisions. In reality the helper is building a database. The summary information needed includes a description of the agency or service, the types of clients it serves, the payment required for the service, the phone number and address, the e-mail address, the URLs for websites, and a contact person. The human service professional may collect information about community services from colleagues, clients, handbooks of agencies, newspapers, professional meetings, the phone book, the Web, and any community service directories produced by other agencies. The Internet has increased the access to information about other agencies, and e-mail and shared databases have facilitated communication between agencies.

Knowing more detailed information about each agency is helpful, including the purpose of the agency, eligibility requirements for services, its location and hours of operation, organizational patterns of staffing, and the nature of the agency funding. Prior to using an agency for referral, a human service professional should know what services it provides, to whom they are provided (individuals or families), whether it uses case management services, and whether it has a good record as a client advocate. Other helpful information includes the qualifications of the staff, their caseload, and their experience with specific populations. The human service professional will have a better knowledge of the agency after visiting the facility to determine its accessibility and its psychological and physical environment. Also critical is knowing how the agency receives referrals, if there is a waiting list, how long a client must wait for services, and what follow-up procedure is used to inform the referring agency of the disposition of the referred client's case. All this requires a detailed understanding of the organization and represents quite a bit of information to gather, but once you have this information, updates can be made with relative ease.

Understanding that creating the file is only one part of building a network, the worker should also begin to make personal contacts with other human service professionals. The worker should then try to establish communication as a cooperative effort—sharing information with other agencies, following up on referrals, and providing feedback to other agencies that have made referrals. These efforts will begin to build the new helper's credibility as a serious professional interested in building and maintaining networks among agencies.

Network building takes time, but it makes the referral process more effective. The better the worker knows the services available, the more appropriate the referrals will be. A network is difficult to maintain: It is a never-ending project, no matter how long the human service professional has been serving the community, because agencies are constantly in flux.

Knowing the Formal and Informal Networks

A network represents informal and formal connections among individuals and agencies within the social service arena. In human service settings, the fabric of the system is formed by the elaborate channels of communication among the agencies and the workers. The securing takes place when both parties confirm that they wish to communicate, engage in two-way communication, and establish channels of communication. Human service delivery is a complex system containing two networks of communication: the formal and the informal. Both must be mastered if professionals are to participate fully in the system.

The formal network consists of organizations such as public and private human service agencies, self-help groups, schools, churches, businesses, and federal, state, and local government agencies. To understand this network, the worker must discover the answers to certain questions: What are the politics of these organizations? Who bears the major responsibilities within each? What are the formal ways to "hook up" the client to the services and resources available?

Beyond the formal network is a valuable informal network that is more difficult to recognize. It is not described in agency policy, formal reporting, or organizational diagrams. It is determined by an established history of agencies working together, personal friendships among workers, and political pressures, and it is maintained by mutual satisfaction and support. The informal network may also include informal helpers such as family and friends who provide needed support. Understanding this informal network is difficult, and accessing it takes time and effort.

There are three types of formal and informal networks: personal, professional, and organizational networks. Personal networks consist of individuals, families, and groups of people who are part of the helper's family or part of his or her social support. Individuals in this context often know the helper very well and can also reach out to a variety of others who can help in the referral process, including people in church, social clubs, and exercise and other activity-based environments. Professional and organizational networks consist of individuals with whom you work and include colleagues, teachers, and supervisors. Networking with these individuals can help reduce duplication and fragmentation of services and eliminate service gaps.

One example of formal and informal networks that human service professionals find in the client population is the formal human service system working to serve African American communities and the formal and informal religious and spirituality communities that support the development of identity, help balance emotions, provide a support system, and maintain overall wellness (Addison-Bradley, Johnson, Sanders,

89

Duncan, & Holcomb-McCoy, 2005; Constantine & Greer, 2003). The focus of spirituality emanates from family tradition and communal connectedness.

A human service worker who wants to help African Americans would need knowledge of the two networks. A special knowledge of the informal system allows the worker to build on the services that are already present rather than duplicate or attempt to replace them with formal services. The worker may learn about the special relationships between helpers in the informal and the formal networks by asking the following questions: What formal services are available? How do the informal and formal systems communicate? Who are the key individuals in both networks who provide services effectively or who assist the elderly in accessing the services?

CHALLENGES IN DAY-TO-DAY HUMAN SERVICE WORK

Human service professionals face many challenges throughout a typical day. They make decisions that affect their work, their clients, and their agencies. How to meet a client's need? What to tell an individual who is ineligible for services? How to stretch resources to cover the needs of three clients rather than one? Whether or not to recommend revocation of parole? At the time, some decisions are serious while others do not seem so serious; they appear to be merely choices about how professionals organize their work and spend their days. Yet, meeting these daily challenges represents survival in the human service world.

Let us examine some of the issues and their potential effects on helping professionals. You will read about the nature of issues such as allocation of resources, paperwork, and turf issues and their impact on human service professionals through the eyes and experiences of Barb LaRosa. She is the human service professional who worked with Almeada and Baby Anne in Chapter 1. She shares her perspective of these challenges and how they impact her work within the human service delivery system. Too many challenges may result in worker encapsulation or burnout. Ms. LaRosa shares her experiences of times when challenges become overwhelming. Professional development is suggested as a strategy that helps professionals meet the challenges they encounter.

ALLOCATION OF RESOURCES

Traditionally, administrators and boards of directors are responsible for allocating resources, such as staff, space, and money. It follows then that direct service professionals are solely involved in providing services once administrators have determined which services are to be provided, and where and to whom they are to be provided. In reality, however, human service professionals are also involved in resource allocation. Often they determine how they will spend their time, how much time they will spend with each client, and which services the client needs or is eligible to receive. Since resources are limited and the demands for resources often exceed their availability in many agencies and organizations, some of the decisions made by human service professionals determine the type of services that each client receives.

When you met Ms. LaRosa in Chapter 1, you were able to see her work with Almeada and appreciate her ability to support Almeada—providing her with information, services, and support during her prenatal care and after the birth of little Anne.

In that chapter the view of Ms. LaRosa was that of Almeada's helper. In the following paragraphs she talks about her own work during the days when Almeada was her client.

Sometimes I think about my job during the time that I met Almeada. I was serving adolescents in the schools and also working with teenage dropouts. In addition, I was providing support for at-home young mothers. I had over 65 girls on my caseload at one time. I tried to keep track of all of them, but it was an impossible task.

I started each day by making a list of everything I had to do. I saw the at-home young mothers weekly for one month, then monthly for six months. Then I would re-evaluate them to see if they could be referred to another service. During that time, the school wanted me to complete an in-depth intake interview with any girl who was pregnant. Then I would develop a plan and make appropriate referrals.

The school referred about four girls to me each week. I tried to see all four the same week they were referred. Finally, I worked with teenage dropouts in a special program that identified irregular attendees who showed potential. I received about 10 referrals a week for this program, both boys and girls. Sometimes I would discover that these girls were pregnant or that the boys were fathers-to-be.

I had two offices, one at the school and one at the welfare agency. I made it a point to begin each day at the school. That way I could check in with the office to see if I could gather any additional information about my clients. Unfortunately, when I began my work at the school, I did not get to hear the early-morning cries for help that I would occasionally receive from my young mothers. I also missed out on the "talk" with my colleagues at the welfare agency. For them, morning was an important time to check in with each other to discuss professional as well as personal business. So what I gained in helping my students at the school, I lost in helping my clients at the welfare office.

The day I received the referral about Almeada, I also received seven other referrals. Almeada was the first student on the list. Taking the first person on the list is a technique of mine that I use to structure my day. I would also review the list of referrals and the list of students left from the day before for crisis situations. I would check with the assistant principal to see if he had any information about the students or if there were any problems that I needed to attend to immediately. I was so alarmed when I first talked with Almeada's parents that I became determined to find her. They told me she was pregnant, and they resented this inconvenience. I knew she needed my help; it was obvious that she had no support from her parents. That afternoon, I found Almeada at the grocery store. I canceled an appointment that evening so that I could meet her after work.

As Ms. LaRosa describes her work, it becomes obvious that she is involved in a daily allocation of her own resources. One resource is time. Like many other helping professionals, she is not able to spend as much time as she would like with each client. She constantly makes decisions about how she allocates her time. In general, she has decided that the pregnant teens and dropouts are a priority, so she spends the mornings of each day seeking them out and helping them plan for the future. When she began to gather information about Almeada, she discovered a very difficult situation. She determined that Almeada needed her immediate attention. She canceled an appointment with another client, so she could begin her work with Almeada. This meant that another client did not receive Ms. LaRosa's services that evening. Ms. LaRosa also describes some of the resources that Almeada received at the expense of some of her other clients.

91

TABLE 8.3	SUMMARY POINTS: ALLOCATION OF RESOURCES

- Resources include staff, buildings, and money.
- Human service professionals are involved in resource allocation.
- When human service professionals determine how they will spend their time, they are involved in resource allocation.
- Decisions about implementation of a client plan also involve resource allocation.
- Special favors, extra attention, or concessions to clients also indicate involvement in resource allocation.

> If you asked me about the most difficult part of my job, I would tell you it's not being able to give my clients all of the services that they need. So many times I discover programs that can serve my students or dropouts, especially the girls. Often though, the girls are not eligible for the services or there are not enough services for all of the girls who need them. I tried to find several options for Almeada to continue her education. I had a friend who ran an evening program, and she made an exception for me to accept Almeada because she did not really have enough credits to qualify for the night classes. In the end Almeada did not participate in the class, but the favor was granted and now I owe my friend the next favor.
>
> I took Almeada to a family-planning clinic. Before the appointment we stopped at a fast-food restaurant to have a soda and talk about the appointment and what she could expect. The school believes that we should not buy our clients food—it is not a rule but a suggestion. The school personnel think that sharing food constitutes "friendly" relationships with students and is a use of time that cannot be documented. Honestly, Almeada was so worried about the appointment that I thought if we could just sit and talk in a place where she felt comfortable, then she might feel better about going. It worked, but it was not time that I could account for in my records.

It is obvious that Almeada received quite a bit of special treatment from Ms. LaRosa and other professionals. Almeada brought an intensity and interest to the helping process, and many professionals worked hard and "bent their rules" to help her. Again, decisions were made to provide Almeada with resources—resources that could have been provided to someone else. Ms. LaRosa "broke" the school suggestion not to take students "out" for lunch or a snack. She is aware that she is violating this protocol but feels that it was absolutely necessary to help Almeada prepare for her appointment at the family-planning clinic.

PAPERWORK BLUES

One demand on a human service professional's time is paperwork. It serves many functions, including providing a permanent record for the services received by the client. This is helpful to any agency employee who works with the client. It documents client history in the human service delivery system and is read by professionals who serve the clients at the same time or in the future. A thorough written record includes an intake interview, a social history, and medical, educational, and mental health records. As this information is obtained and carefully read by the helper, it also becomes a vehicle for organizing what is known about the client and what services are needed. In some cases, this organization may lead to possible solutions.

Paperwork involves a record of referrals and case notes of any client–helper contacts. It also documents the time that has been spent by an agency or professional, which is used for billing and accountability audits. Paperwork is becoming increasingly important in this time of strict professional accountability and scarce resources. Work with insurance and managed care companies has not only intensified and complicated the need for paperwork but has also created additional work for each professional who struggles with managing it all. If an agency is receiving state funds or support from a granting foundation, records are used in the evaluation process. Records provide documentation of the benefits of the work to clients and the community.

Clearly, the task of doing the paperwork signifies less time for client contact. Ms. LaRosa struggles with this problem.

> I have always liked to do my paperwork. Most of my co-workers do not like it and procrastinate. When I do my paperwork, it gives me a time to think about my clients, their problems, and how I can help them. I will admit that some of the paperwork drives me crazy, especially when I have to fill out multiple forms with the same information. Computers make the paperwork easier, although someone still has to enter the information. When I worked with Almeada, the paperwork actually became a nightmare for me because her case was complicated. Since I was working in three programs, I had to keep three sets of records, and all three were different. Sometimes I would try to complete one form for the right person in the wrong program. I would catch myself before I wasted too much time. Because I had two offices, it was also difficult to always have the information and records that I needed at the right office.

Each professional learns the importance of paperwork. Knowing how to handle it is a skill and a responsibility. Some helpers are very well organized, and they manage their paperwork successfully and still see a large number of clients. For most, the nature of the job, with its crises and unexpected client requests, works against any set time for paperwork. The best plans are often left unfulfilled. There is no doubt that the paperwork takes valuable time that could be used with the client. To solve that problem, human service professionals often take their paperwork home, working long after hours so that they can spend more time with their clients. They then shortchange themselves on time to focus on self, family, and others. Some helpers shorten the time they spend on paperwork, not being as thorough as they might. Incomplete or spotty records do not help the agency or the client in the long run. Still others take the time to keep excellent records and accept this as part of the job, but then they have less client contact.

Turf Issues

Within the context of the human service delivery system, there is a tension between competition and coalition building among agencies. For the most part, within communities, human service professionals find cooperation and goodwill among agencies as all strive together to meet common goals. This is a positive environment for human service professionals to work together for the good of the client. At times, however, either underlying tension or open conflict exists among organizations.

93

TABLE 8.4	SUMMARY POINTS: THE IMPORTANCE OF PAPERWORK

- Paperwork has a variety of functions that include establishing a permanent client record, documenting client history, writing important assessments and reports, documenting referrals and billing units, and providing a record for accountability purposes.

- Professionals determine how much time and effort will go into their paperwork and report writing.

- Intensive time spent with paperwork means less time with clients.

This tension, commonly referred to as a dispute over **"turf,"** occurs for several reasons. Sometimes an agency operates in a competitive mode and sees other agencies as competing for the same resources and clients. This competition often occurs when more than one for-profit agency competes for clients; each believes there is room for only one or a few human service agencies to prosper. There are also times when an agency sees no real benefit from cooperating with another agency; it may believe there will be a loss of benefits for the organization. Because flexibility with each agency is essential for cooperation, an agency may not be able to cooperate because its mission and goals cannot change fast enough to work collaboratively. Finally, an agency may simply mistrust the intentions of those with whom they are working (Children's Alliance, 2006).

Working together becomes even more difficult when turf issues become turf battles. Strife in the human service sector can erupt over issues of inequality. For example, sometimes collaboration appears to benefit one agency more than another or one organization has access to more resources. Sometimes agencies feel they are dedicated to serving a particular area or a targeted population, and they are unwilling to share that responsibility. Agencies may also believe that the collaborative effort leads them away from their own mission and goals. Other times agencies do not agree on the methods to solve particular social problems. Finally, personality issues among individuals representing different agencies may interfere with the collaborative effort (Peck & Hague, 2006).

Ms. LaRosa has been involved in collaborative work throughout her career. Here she shares some of her experiences.

> For the most part, my experience with other agencies has been positive, since I usually work at the local level. What I mean by that is I contact other workers for help, and I help them in turn. I consider these people my colleagues. Sometimes we talk with each other every day, and other times we don't have contact for over a year. But usually we are always ready to help one another. Let me give you several examples that we have already talked about. My friend who runs the night classes and I maintain weekly contact. Sometimes I am able to help her with clients, and other times she is able to help me.
>
> I try to avoid the politics at the higher levels of agency work. The family planning clinic is a good example. I know that the superintendent of schools and his assistant tried working with five clinics in town to establish a coalition for teen pregnancy. The effort failed. My friend was able to tell the story from her perspective.
>
> She said that her boss opposed the mission of two of the clinics that were going to be in the collaborative. The first priority for those clinics is to promote adoption. They will not provide information about abortion, even when asked. They have a

94

TABLE 8.5	SUMMARY POINTS: TURF ISSUES

- Collaboration among agencies benefits clients and the community.
- Turf issues arise among agencies over resources, power, and political issues.
- Turf issues can become turf battles and diminish opportunities for collaboration.
- Collaborative efforts are complex and need attention and continuous communication.

waiting list of clients who want babies, and they provide adoption services in concert with family planning. Evidently when the five clinics sat around the table, the issues of mission and goals were raised immediately. One director left the meeting early; the remainder continued to meet with the superintendent. At the end of the meeting, those present decided that no collaborative could be formed; each family planning clinic formalized individualized partnerships with the school system.

Of course I have some really positive examples to share. When I called Mr. Alvarez at the Department of Human Services (DHS), he was able to help Almeada right away because of the partnerships his organization had formed with several employers. In fact, they had formed the partnerships under the umbrella of the Chamber of Commerce and the City Development Council. That meant they did not have to form multiple partnerships; the Chamber and the Development Council, representing over 60 businesses, guaranteed cooperation among its members. Mr. Alvarez says that he has been able to provide vocational services much more effectively than ever before.

Ms. LaRosa provides two examples for us, one in which a collaborative effort was undermined by turf issues and one where a partnership was formed for the benefit of clients within the city. Agencies and organizations, human service professionals, clients, and the community all benefit when coalitions exist. Because the relationships are complex, continuous communication about goals, methods, and attention to turf issues helps resolve turf issues before they become turf battles.

Often, working within the human service delivery context can be very challenging. Professionals confront difficult issues every day; at times the organizational setting supports the human service work; at other times the bureaucracy contributes to the stress. Let us look at what happens to helpers when they face too many challenges.

ENCAPSULATION AND BURNOUT

Working as a human service professional is challenging and rewarding. Unfortunately, the enthusiasm can fade as workers become disenchanted, experience disequilibrium, and behave in ways that are less than professional. One reaction to the stresses and strains experienced by workers in helping professions is **encapsulaton**—retreating from the engagement of helping and becoming rigid, insensitive, uncaring professionals. Another result of the pressures of the job may be burnout, a syndrome that can result in poor work performance or a decision to leave the profession.

Helpers who become encapsulated may become static in their work as they face the difficulties of working within the human service delivery system. They may feel so threatened and frightened by the difficult tasks they are asked to perform that they quit

95

learning, growing, and trying—thus becoming encapsulated. Such workers relate to clients in characteristic ways. First, they become rigid and inflexible, believing that there are enduring truths that must be upheld. Such truths can take many forms, such as "The system's rules are always right and just" or "Individuals who are unemployed do not deserve to be helped." If human service professionals are dynamic, their personal and professional experiences continually modify their ideas about clients and the entire delivery system. They grow, learning about the system and how it operates as well as learning about self. Clinging to the "truths" workers have at the beginning of their professional careers limits what they can learn from their experiences.

Ms. LaRosa talks about a time when she was encapsulated as a worker. She learned a lot during this time and believes that she is now a more committed professional as a result of the experience.

> Earlier I talked about my incredible schedule and workload. What I did not talk about was how much I enjoy my work. Working with adolescents is a great job. The preceding year, though, was a time of professional crisis for me. At this point I am able to see how much I have grown as a professional. Because I was once fairly rigid, today it is almost impossible to believe that I could have been an effective helper.
>
> I had been working with teenagers in a girl and boys club setting. I was so excited about my work when I began. I would get up and head to work at 7 A.M. just to be the first person in the building. By the time the young children arrived at 7:30 A.M., I was ready for them. I became involved in the lives of many of the families of my clients and worried about each and every one of them. I was also absolutely sure about what was best for them. I came from a wonderful family and was raised by loving parents. I was appalled by what I thought was inadequate and sometimes frightening care. Many of the parents were not at home for their children; babies were left with older siblings while parents worked. Single mothers were raising as many as five or six children. Some parents had extreme ways of disciplining their children. I tried to change the behaviors of these parents and became so frustrated when they refused to change.
>
> When I look back now, I think the only thing that saved my relationship with these parents was my absolute dedication to helping them. They knew they could depend upon me, even if I was constantly trying to show them a better way to raise their children. But, by the end of the school year, I really did not like the parents. I was not sure they deserved my attention since they were not changing their ways.

Encapsulated workers depend only on their own personal experiences and frames of references, which limits their understanding of their clients. Ms. LaRosa illustrates this limited understanding. There are many different types of clients and client situations, and it is difficult to be familiar with all of them. As a result, helping professionals should constantly read, discuss, and observe clients, so they can broaden the base from which they understand clients' experiences. Professionals who do not expand their knowledge remain limited in the ways in which they can serve their clients.

As mentioned, another result of the stress and strain new professionals experience is burnout. This condition results from negative changes in attitudes and behavior that are precipitated by job strain (Weiten & Lloyd, 2003). Like encapsulation, burnout effects the day-to-day work of the professional and results in behavior that has negative effects on the work environment as well as the helping process. There are identifiable pressures that lead to burnout. Loss of idealism and disappointment in

TABLE 8.6	SUMMARY POINTS: ENCAPSULATION AND BURNOUT

Encapsulation occurs when:

- Professionals become static in their work;
- Professionals become rigid and inflexible and uphold their own beliefs or truths;
- Professionals support the beliefs of the traditional culture; and
- Clients are asked to accept norms of the traditional culture.

Burnout occurs when:

- There are multiple pressures at work over a long period of time;
- Professionals have unrealistic expectations about their job outcomes;
- Professionals begin to miss work, arrive late, denigrate their clients; and
- The bureaucracy does not support the professional or the client.

client motivations may result in a loss of commitment to both job and clients. Professionals who experience burnout may also be reacting to a less-than-perfect work setting—one that is too demanding, too frustrating, or too boring.

Some symptoms of burnout are a change in attitude about work, lower expectations of performance, severe emotional detachment from work, reduced psychological involvement with clients, and an intense concern with self. With burnout, helpers are likely to perceive work more negatively, resulting in sick days, tardiness, and clock watching. The syndrome also affects how workers perceive clients. They may call them names behind their backs, become angry with them, or feel that they are irresponsible and ungrateful for the help that is given them. These behaviors all impact negatively on the helper's ability to assist the client. They violate many of the basic values of helping, such as tolerance and acceptance of the client. In addition, individuals who are themselves involuntary clients are less likely to respond positively or see helpers in a positive light.

There are also some physical symptoms of burnout, such as chronic fatigue, frequent colds, serious illness, stomach trouble, lower back pain, and perhaps even substance abuse. Burnout may also affect the person's relationships with others outside of work, and the helper may be unable to take up new hobbies or concentrate on anything for long periods of time.

Ms. LaRosa has only experienced periodic burnout, but she has worked with a number of professionals who have severe cases of the syndrome. During the time she was working with Almeada, she had many of the symptoms. It was because she had such a large caseload and worked such long hours. Although she was never late or tardy, she began to resent her work. She would complain about her job to her friends and family, but she never took it out on her clients, or so she thought. Ms. LaRosa had begun to notice little things that denoted signs of burnout. As a result, she tried to adjust her pattern of unrealistic expectations for each workday. It is easy to lose your sense of professionalism when work demands exceed energy and resources.

97

Burnout is not temporary strain but rather a pattern of being and thinking that cannot easily be interrupted unless specific efforts are made to alleviate it. It is not just "poor adjustment" that can be corrected easily. Recovery from burnout is a long process that necessitates many changes in the life and work of the professionals who are affected.

PROFESSIONAL DEVELOPMENT

One approach that counters the devastating effects of encapsulation and burnout is professional development. In fact, this is a positive approach to address the challenges that affect the day-to-day work of helpers. A commitment to professional development is a means of keeping positively engaged and well-supported while delivering services.

Critical to improving one's professional standing is a commitment to developing new knowledge and skills. The ultimate goal is to be a more effective helper and to be able to respond to each helping opportunity in a way that positively supports the client. If the helper is involved in learning new knowledge about clients, developing and improving skills, and reflecting on current practice, then the services he or she is delivering are more effective. Within the field of human services, new information is always available about the problems of clients' experiences. New methodologies are constantly being developed to help professionals address client needs. As the field of human service delivery constantly changes, professionals need to assess what these changes mean for their work with clients. Professional development means helpers do not serve clients in the same way, year after year, but recognize that their clients' problems change, the world in which they live shifts, and new ways of helping continually emerge.

Both formal and informal approaches to continuing education are important to professional growth. Returning to school for an advanced degree—whether it be an associate, baccalaureate, master's, doctorate, or specialist degree—is a legitimate way to continue professional education in the human services. Such formal education will also open alterative career paths and allow helpers to increase their qualifications and competence. Workshops and conferences are also available within an organization or within the working radius of the professional to broaden his or her understanding of client needs and the changing times. Other educational opportunities may focus on developing one or two specific skills in greater depth. Ms. LaRosa shares with us her own experiences with professional development.

I am indebted to a summer educational experience I had when I worked with the boys and girls club. My fellow students allowed me to see the "client experience" from another perspective. As they talked about their work with helpers and their frustrations with the helping process, I felt shame for the way in which I had treated the parents with whom I had worked. But we learned in class how to avoid treating clients in such a disrespectful way, so I was able to replace one set of thoughts and behaviors with another. Since that summer, I have continued to believe that professional development is a critical part of becoming a professional.

Sometimes it is easy to be involved in professional development. Other times it seems impossible to take the time to attend a workshop, lecture, or class. I know the times that I think I am too busy to go are the very times that I should quit what I am

98

doing and sign up for that seminar or workshop. I am always so glad once I am there. There is an excitement I feel when I am involved in learning. It is also a good way to share ideas with other professionals and to expand my professional network. The last workshop that I attended was three months ago. The focus was substance abuse, which is a common problem among my clients. I learned how the very latest brain research impacts the ways in which we now deliver treatment to this population. Three professionals I met at the workshop volunteered to establish a "group counseling" experience for my pregnant girls.

Commitment to the profession is also a part of professional development. When human service professionals become active in an organization or become active members of the community, they expand their professional associations and their professional awareness. Anytime they study political issues or become deeply involved in solving individual or community problems that are difficult to comprehend, they are expanding their professional understanding. Even the continuous updating of their knowledge of the community, its professionals, and its resources is an informal professional development process.

PROMOTING CHANGE IN A DYNAMIC WORLD

One continuous theme throughout this text is that the world is changing rapidly. We are experiencing the globalization of the economy, increased immigration, the development of new technologies, and the emergence of new methodologies for approaching the problems in this third millennium. For a human service professional to be effective with and responsive to clients, and knowledgeable about and sensitive to community needs, it is increasingly important to function as a change agent. Becoming involved in change is often difficult for the beginning professional.

This section will present three contexts in which professionals can promote change. The first is within the arena of the local community, becoming involved in developing specific services in response to community needs. The second is also within the context of the community, initiating and participating in **community organizing**. The focus on this type of change occurs with the development of a new vision or a new focus for the community. Community organizing occurs when the development of a coalition of individuals and communities is powerful enough to continue to create and promote change. The third approach centers around the **empowerment** of a specific population with little previous status or power. The empowerment occurs once the population is identified and a team of professionals and other interested individuals work with that population to build the skills that allow them to advocate for themselves and facilitate their own change. A description and examples of each of these three approaches follow.

DEVELOPING SERVICES IN RESPONSE TO HUMAN NEEDS

In developing, maintaining, and reevaluating human service delivery, a primary consideration is the response to community needs. The community has a dual role in the causation and resolution of client problems. On one hand, the community is a source of client problems. On the other hand, it provides many of the resources needed for resolving problems. The World Bank announced a project beginning in 2007 to

empower women in developing countries as a way of addressing community needs (World Bank, 2006). The project links women's economic power with education, reduction of infant mortality, improved health, and the reduction of HIV/AIDS. Two issues, advocacy for nonexistent services and planning based on community needs, are integral components of fostering change.

Advocating the establishment of services that are nonexistent is one of the most difficult responsibilities of the human service professional. The **advocate** is one who speaks up for the rights of others and defends those who cannot defend themselves. When helpers discover that their clients have needs that cannot be met through the human service delivery system, they have a responsibility to work with others to develop alternative ways of meeting those needs. To do so requires skills that incorporate working with the individual, agencies, and legal and legislative bodies. Regardless of the type of advocacy, the process is much the same:

- Identify the needs of the individual or the population.
- Determine how to meet the needs.
- Work with a network of individuals or agencies to provide the services.
- Identify the barriers that must be overcome.

100

BOX 8.3	INTERNATIONAL FOCUS
	World Bank: Gender Equity as Smart Economics

The World Bank is working to address the economic needs of women in developing countries. The focus is on working with countries, donors, and other development agencies to further the economic empowerment of women by encouraging women's participation in government and business infrastructures, finance, and agriculture. The project also supports research about the factors that restrict gender equity and those that encourage women's participation in the economic sector. One story that illustrates the power of economic involvement comes from the island of Char Montaz, Bangladesh.

Women in this small and isolated island, with funding and support from the World Bank and the United Nations, began a small company whose goal was to create battery-powered lamps. The women, defying the long-held custom of women remaining in the home, built these lamps to use in the home, replacing kerosene lanterns and reducing pollution. This effort resulted in the usage of over 1,000 lamps, businesses remaining open longer, more children staying in school, and incomes increasing over 30%.

The World Bank believes that the programs will reflect the needs of each country. For example, in many countries women are more educated that ever before, but they are still having difficulty finding jobs

so they can support themselves. Because there is a strong link between women's economic status and poverty, level of education, health, and infant mortality, the World Bank's directors believe that this project, by creating opportunities for women, will help eradicate poverty in developing countries. Some specific objectives the World Bank has targeted for this project include:

- Providing the women access to financial services and business education
- Providing women with school-to-work transition training
- Providing women with legal training to understand both women's issues and economic issues
- Teaching women technical skills needed for their businesses, whether small industry or agriculturally related
- Supporting the revision of discriminatory laws that restrict women's economic activity

Source: Adapted from the *World Bank: Empowering women, boosting economies.* (2006, October 4). Retrieved November 11, 2006, from http://web.worldbank.org/WBSITE/EXTERNAL/NEWS/0,contentMDK:21079590~menuPK:34457~pagePK:34370~piPK:34424~theSitePK:4607,00.html

- Teach clients about the advocacy process and give them a role.
- Negotiate to meet goals and objectives.
- Develop a framework that continues the success of the advocacy process.

Many professionals are successful in acting as advocates for their individual clients and can use their networking skills to find food where no food services exist, glasses and other special medical needs where resources are unavailable, and housing for those who temporarily need shelter. More difficult is the advocacy as an individual that involves developing a political voice for the larger issues that require community, state, or national attention. Colin Powell's championing of America's Promise and the lobbying efforts of Nancy Reagan and Michael J. Fox for funding for stem cell research are examples of advocacy in the community, state, and national arenas for issues of concern.

A critical component in developing services is knowing both the needs and the characteristics of the populations in need. The following case study illustrates the importance of being able to identify the problems and develop programs that address those specific problems when planning for services. A change project in Redwood City, California, did just that.

Community organizers in this mid-size city near San Francisco were interested in improving the lives of youth who lived in their community. They had always worked from a community collaboration model, but when it came to identifying the needs of the youth in their community, they realized that they were not clear what those needs were. Not only would they ask these youth what they needed, they also involved the youth in the data gathering process.

To begin the project, they asked eighth graders to help them collect information about the youth in their city using the research methods that they were learning in their social science classes. The youth would then help design programs and evaluate them. In other words, their involvement would span the entire life of the program. These middle school students would work with adults from community organizations and schools to develop services and programs to meet the needs identified.

The interviews that the middle school students collected surprised the adult participants of the project. Instead of just raising youth-related issues, these young interviewers uncovered a concern for broader community issues among their interviewees. For example, the youth talked about the lack of fun in their communities and wished they had some place to just hang out and be with each other. But they also talked about the high cost of food and housing, little access to transportation, and violence.

The youthful participants were able to contribute to the dialogue about the planning and programming to address the issues identified. And they advocated for services that would help other populations, not just themselves. Specific recommendations included concrete suggestions for improving the community, such as an archway ramp across a busy street so that all members of the neighborhood could cross without harm. They also asked for broader participation in the political process. (Fernandez, 2002, pp. 1–8).

Suppose you are a human service professional planning services to reduce youth-related violence in your city or rural area. What needs must be considered? How would you discover what those needs are? What problems might you anticipate in implementing new programs in the community? What actions might you take to ensure successful planning and implementation?

In answering these questions, you may realize how difficult planning is. Your responses should consider a variety of viewpoints and take into consideration how the services fit within the context of the current environment.

ORGANIZING TO PROMOTE COMMUNITY CHANGE

Promoting community change relies on the development and use of a network or larger confederation to advance the cause, mobilize individuals and agencies in the community, and create a financial resource base and a willing workforce of professionals and volunteers. Although promoting community change is a broader activity than just creating services, the change that you want to create must be defined, and numerous issues could benefit from the effort and focus. Read any national or local newspaper, listen to conversations between friends, tape dialogues in a teacher's lounge, or monitor the exchanges in a human service agency and organization lounge. In all of these settings you will hear numerous issues being raised. Unfortunately, most of these communications end with frustration, hopelessness, some humor, but no hope for action. The difficulties seem too challenging to overcome. (See Table 8.7).

102

BOX 8.4	WEB SOURCES
	Find Out More about Community Organizing

http://uac.utoledo.edu/Links/comdev.htm

This comprehensive community organizing on-line site is housed at the University of Toledo. The mission of this organization is to help connect people who care about the craft of community organizing. This organization is also committed to finding and providing information that organizers and scholars can use to learn, teach, and do community organizing.

http://www.uwm.edu:80/Library/arch/findaids/mss011.htm

This website provides a fascinating history of a community organizing effort in Milwaukee, Wisconsin, that of the Eastside Housing Action Committee. The records of activities were kept from 1972 to 1978.

http://www.gamaliel.org/

This is the website of The Gamaliel Foundation, originally established in 1968 to support the Contract Buyers League, an organization in the African-American community on Chicago's West Side. The league was fighting to protect homeowners who had bought their homes on contract because financial institutions had red-lined the area. In 1986, the foundation was revamped as an organizing institute, with a mission to support grassroots leaders in their efforts to build and maintain empowerment organizations in low-income communities. The purpose of this website is to link those in need with existing community organizing resources.

http://www.grassrootsworks.net/

GrassRoots Organizing Works is an organization that supports the development of volunteer organizing for low income individuals and people of color. This organization supports target organizations and works with them on a two-year cycle to foster community development skills and projects.

http://www.cfls1.org

Community Family Life Services in Washington, D.C., is active in making changes within the environments of those in need. The CFLS Community Organizing Program develops and implements strategies for neighborhood participation and revitalization in low-income sections of Washington, D.C. Working closely with the residents and housing developers in the Galveston Place and Brandywine Street neighborhoods in Ward 8, CFLS has helped residents take pride in and take charge of their communities.

TABLE 8.7	PRINCIPLES OF COMMUNITY ORGANIZING

- Individuals and organizations identify a common goal.
- Like-minded individuals and organizations consolidate themselves to have a more effective voice in the community.
- All individual members of the community are welcome to participate in the effort, including politicians, business leaders, citizens, and others.
- Organizations and agencies are welcome to form a network of the concerned. This network includes schools, financial institutions, social service organizations, political organizations, nonprofit organizations, and others.
- The combined effort of many voices has the power to facilitate change.
- Basic to the work is organizing as a team and gathering information to understand the community and its needs.
- Basic to the work is developing an action plan.

The process of community action begins with a community action plan (CAP). The Presidents' Summit for America's Future prepared material that outlines the steps in developing a community action plan (America's Promise, 2006). It is during the development of this plan that the concerned coalition answers the question "How will this initiative be carried out?" To answer that question fully, the following questions adapted from the America's Promise plans for promoting change (America's Promise):

- What will be the community effort focus?
- Where can we find the resources we need?
- What knowledge and skills do we need to support our effort?
- What offices, technology, and equipment do we need?
- How will we gather support?
- What are the benefits of being in this coalition?
- How do we promote ourselves?

The CAP will address these questions, develop a plan of action, make assignments, and create a timeline to ensure that the plan will be implemented.

The development of the CAP focuses on meeting the goals and objectives. It begins to bring people together to talk about issues. For the first time, individuals from every corner of the community are talking together. The action plan becomes the forum for the conversation; a strong community network is being built. Not all conversation has to occur when individuals are meeting together. There are new models of community organizing that use technology to bring people together to discuss major issues and develop CAPs. These programs are developed to teach organizers how to effectively use technology to allow individuals in remote areas to participate in the community action process.

In summary, work within the community to promote change is an important part of the human service professional's responsibility. It can be a rewarding way to improve client environments and services and can expand the helper's network to include many individuals and organizations outside the human service.

USING A MODEL OF CLIENT EMPOWERMENT

Throughout this text we have discussed the importance of both advocacy for the client and empowerment of the client. Using a model of client empowerment is another approach to facilitating change, a model that is commonly used in many developing countries. The primary goal of this model is to ultimately place the advocacy and empowerment in the hands and voices of the clients or those in need. The basic thrust of this model is to educate and train those in need to organize, establish their agenda, and work for their own cause by organizing campaigns, networking with government and business leaders, proposing legislation, and participating in the political, economic, and social processes of the community. How does an effort like this begin?

One such example is the Women's Bean Project (WBP), a not-for-profit effort begun 16 years ago in Denver, Colorado. It is an on-site packaged food business (Haynes, Ryan, & MacDonald, 2006).

104

TABLE 8.8	SUMMARY POINTS: PROMOTING CHANGE

- Promoting change is an important role for the human service professional.

- One way of supporting change is to develop services in response to community needs, including establishing services that are nonexistent.

- The process to promote change involves identifying needs, deciding how needs can best be met, working with a network of individuals or agencies to provide services, identifying barriers that must be overcome, and teaching clients the advocacy process.

- Negotiating the meeting of goals and objectives and developing plans for future services are also part of the process.

- Community involvement to promote change uses a confederation of individuals and organizations committed to the same cause.

- One model of client empowerment focuses almost entirely on supporting clients to develop their own agenda, support structure, plan for change and evaluation, and the recruitment of new members.

This project prepares women for the world of work by teaching them basic job skills and basic life skills. Each woman commits to enrollment in the project for at least six months and for as long as a year. Women with backgrounds of chronic poverty and unemployment are eligible to enroll. Success stories include Mary, who kicked a 2-year old heroin addiction, left prison, and is now a productive worker and an involved grandparent for the children she wasn't able to care for. Or Barbara who came to the Bean Project when she was living in a homeless shelter and had no job skills to help her obtain employment and has now been employed at the same place for seven years. She owns a home and a car (Haynes et al., 2006).

The WBP uses the Results Oriented Management and Accountability (ROMA) method that helps link project goals to outcomes, indicates measures of success, and demands a data collection and data analysis process. In line with the commitment to empowerment and advocacy, the agency itself has changed with its use of ROMA. Successes include participants who focus on improving their lives, an increased graduation rate in the program and an increased in the rate of employment. The program offers women an opportunity to develop skills, stabilize their lives, and in turn begin to help others. (Haynes et al., 2006)

There are many ways the human service worker can become involved in change. You do not have to spearhead a movement or fight single handedly for your clients. Just look around your neighborhood, city, or organization to find efforts you wish to support to ultimately improve the lives and environments of your clients.

KEY TERMS

advocate	empowerment	network	referral
brokering	encapsulation	organizational chart	resources
chain of command	job description	organizational climate	turf
community organizing	mission	privatization	

105

BOX 8.5	INTERNATIONAL FOCUS
	Disha Kendra

Disha Kendra was established in 1978 by Jagrut Bhaubandhi Sangatana to help village tribal people in India fight their socioeconomic and political oppression. Tribals are indigenous people who live in remote rural areas in India. Each tribe has a different culture, speaks a unique dialect, and lives according to long-standing traditions.

The first phase of the organization's work (1978–1983) focused on economic and human rights development. One example of this work was the two-year process of breaking the economic hold of the moneylender on the 35-household village of Chadhawadi and substituting a six-year bank-loan program to support local farming efforts. During this initial phase, education was also enhanced with the formation of preschool and adult education programs. From 1983 to 1991—the second and third phases of the organization's history—the effort determined long- and short-term needs of the village and assessed the outcomes of past efforts. In addition, the organization promoted the tribal people's ability to lead their own political organizations as they struggled to increase the availability of water, electricity, and employment opportunities.

The fourth phase of the agency's work is underway and includes strengthening political organization and leadership training, improving community organization, and improving the lives of tribal women. The emphasis is on helping tribals help themselves.

During the authors' visit to the village, the agency's political action director, Bunsi, conducted a meeting of the village committee, a group of six men from surrounding villages. Their task was to prepare for a meeting the following week with the police superintendent inspector who would rule on a land-access dispute. A wealthy Mumbai businessman had bought a large track of land near the village and was denying access to their farmland, water supply, and firewood. Bunsi asked those in attendance to decide who would speak for the committee, and he explained the hearing process. They then role-played what the spokesman would say at the hearing.

The agency workers visit the villages weekly or live in the villages themselves. They are available to help with whatever issues arise that affect the rights of tribals as a protected class of people in India.

THINGS TO REMEMBER

1. The work of the human service professional occurs within an agency or organization.

2. An agency's written mission statement communicates an agency's purpose by summarizing its guiding principles.

3. Goal statements, job descriptions, and policies and procedures are other agency documents that clarify the work of an agency and its employers.

4. The relationships among the individuals who work in an agency and the departments to which they are assigned describe an agency's structure.

5. Chain of command, often illustrated by an organizational chart, refers to the layers of authority in an agency.

6. Funding sources determine if an agency is public or governmental, not for-profit (voluntary), or for-profit.

7. Human service agencies exist within the context of a community that influences agency operations, services, clients, and professionals.

8. One of the most important roles of a human service professional is brokering, or referring a client to another agency or service.

106

9. The referral process involves the worker, the client, and the other agency to which the client is referred.

10. In referral, the beginning human service professional is at a disadvantage because of a lack of experience in the system, a lack of personal contacts with workers in the system, and a lack of knowledge about the many problems that clients may have.

11. The beginning professional must develop a systematic way of building a file of information about the human services network for referral purposes.

12. Challenges such as allocation of resources, paperwork, and turf issues influence the work of the human service professional.

13. Responses such as encapsulation and burnout leave workers unable to be effective helpers.

14. Professional development strategies such as attending workshops and participating in professional organizations help professionals respond to changes in human services.

15. An important responsibility of the human service professional is to be an advocate for change.

16. In developing, maintaining, and reevaluating the delivery of human services, it is important to consider human services as a response to community needs.

17. Empowering clients to advocate for their own change is one model of responding to client needs.

ADDITIONAL READINGS: FOCUS ON ORGANIZATIONS

Bolman, L. G., & Deal, T. E. (2003). *Reframing organizations: Artistry, choice, and leadership.* San Francisco: Jossey-Bass.
A consistent bestseller, this book offers practical ways of thinking about today's challenges.

Homan, M. S. (2004). *Rules of the game: Lessons from the field of community change.* Pacific Grove, CA: Brooks/Cole.
The author offers practical wisdom and 135 guidelines for community change as readers explore what they need to know about themselves, others, and the change process.

Hull, G. H., & Kirst-Ashman, K. K. (2004). *Generalist practice with organizations and communities.* Belmont, CA: Wadsworth.
This text applies the generalist practice model to work with larger systems, including organizations, neighborhoods, and communities.

Sen, R. (2003). *Stir it up: Lessons in community organizing and advocacy.* Hoboken, NJ: Jossey-Bass.
This text provides the steps of building a constituency and organizing for social justice. There are multiple case studies to illustrate the concepts presented.

Smith, M. B., Graham, Y., & Guttmacher, S. (2005). *Community-based health organizations: Advocating for improved health.* New Brunswick, NJ: Jossey-Bass.
This text presents basic principles to create community-based health organizations. Included is a history of community-based care and a structured outline of developing services in communities.

REFERENCES

Addison-Bradley, C., Johnson, D., Sanders, J. L., Duncan, L., & Holcomb-McCoy, C. (2005 January). Forging a collaborative relationship between the black church and the counseling profession. *Counseling and Values, 49,* 147–154. Retrieved November 11, 2006, from Academic Search Premier.

Aging with Dignity. (2006). *Home.* Retrieved October 11, 2006, from http://www.agingwithdignity.org/.

107

America's Promise. (2006). *Home*. Retrieved November 11, 2006, from http://www.americaspromise.org/.

Bureau of Labor Statistics. (2006). *Health*. Retrieved November 11, 2006, from http://www.bls.gov/oco/cg/cgs035.htmhttp://www.bls.gov/oco/cg/cgs035.htm.

Children's Alliance. (2006). *Voice of Washington's children, youth and families*. Retrieved November 11, 2006, from http://www.childrensalliance.org/.

Constantine, M. G., & Greer, T. M. (2003). Personal, academic, and career counseling of African American women in college settings. In M. Howard-Hamilton (Ed.), *Meeting the needs of African American women: New directions for student services* (pp. 41–51). San Francisco: Jossey-Bass.

Fernandez, M. A. (2002). *Creating community change: Challenges and tensions in community youth research*. Palo Alto, CA: John W. Gardner Center for Youth and Their Communities.

Haynes, S., Ryan, T., & MacDonald, B. (2006). *The Women's Bean Project: Defining the mission and measuring outcomes to better serve the needs of women*. Unpublished manuscript, Denver, Colorado.

Homan, M. (2004). *Promoting community change* (3rd ed.). Pacific Grove, CA: Brooks/Cole.

Lewis, J. A., Lewis, M. D., Packard, T., & Souflee, F. (2006). *Management of human service programs* (3rd ed.). Pacific Grove, CA: Brooks/Cole.

Peck, G. P., & Hague, C. E. (2006). *Turf issues* (CDFS 12). Retrieved November 11, 2006 from http://ohioline.osu.edu/bc-fact/0012.html.

Social Support Center. (2006). *Community policing department*. Abu Dhabi, United Arab Emirates Ministry of Interior, Abu Dhabi Police G. H. Q.

Weiten, W., & Lloyd, M. (2003). *Psychology applied to modern life: Adjustment in the 21st century* (7th ed.). Belmont, CA: Wadsworth.

World Bank. (2006). *Gender equality as smart economics: A World Bank Group Gender Action Plan*. Retrieved November 11, 2006, from http://siteresources.worldbank.org/INTGENDER/Resources/GAPQ&AOct5.pdf.